FROM HIGHRISE TO HAYSTACK

sylviane duval

Enjoy!
Sylviane

FIRST PRINTING

Canadian Cataloguing in Publication Data

Duval, Sylviane
From Highrise To Haystack

ISBN 0-9738217-0-1

To order more copies: **www.sylvianeduval.ca**

Back cover photography: Michael Komendat
Cover design: Accurate Design and Communication Inc., Ottawa
Copy editing: Connie Munro
Interior design and layout: Sylviane Duval
Website maintenance: Sylviane Duval
Produced in Canada: Gilmore Printing Services Inc., Ottawa

When Sylviane Duval attended Lucie Clayton College for Young Ladies in London, England, she never imagined that she would give up her stylish, high-heeled pumps for manure-encrusted rubber boots or plant row upon row of tiny carrot seeds on her hands and knees in the mud.

Armed with a dream of growing organic vegetables, Sylviane exchanged the whirlwind life of downtown Montreal in 1998 in favour of a run-down hobby farm in Eastern Ontario. Although the farm operation was short-lived, the rural lifestyle stimulated her creative juices.

Sylviane makes her living as a freelance writer. A regular, creative columnist for *Organic Earth Magazine*, she also writes functional texts for public sector and government clients. Just before he retired from the CBC, Arthur Black read one of her short stories on his *Basic Black* show.

When she doesn't have a garden spade or pen in hand, she makes bobbin lace.

Sylviane shares her life with her partner, three cats, a German Shepherd and four horses.

❧

contents

*Go confidently in the direction of
your dreams. Live the life you've imagined.*
Henry David Thoreau (1817 – 1862)

acknowledgements

To Tony, my unconventional and stubborn partner, magnet to the quirks of life.

To George McIntosh for having faith in me.

To Lynn-Marie Holland, Kay Johnston and France Jodoin for the little things that mean so much.

To Doug McKercher of Fomorian Press for guiding me through some tough decisions.

To Brenda Adams of Accurate Design and Communication Inc. and Thomas Smith of Gilmore Printing Services Inc. for going out of their way to help an ant climb a mountain.

To everyone who, willingly or unwittingly, supported my literary efforts.

the welcome-to-farmin' years

.

decision time

I remember the day time stood still. October 31, 1995. Halloween.

"What's wrong with everybody?" asked my colleague, Liz LaFlamme. She was dressed as a particularly grisly murder victim. "Someone asked me if I was all right—if I needed to get to hospital!"

Unusually enough for McGill University, where we both worked at a research institute within the Electrical Engineering department, nobody—but *nobody*—was in costume. Any other year, the campus would be a riot of zombies, witches and Trekkies.

"D'you think I look all right?" she continued, examining her outfit. "I'm supposed to look dead. If *I* was really all right, then I wouldn't look dead. On the other hand, if my *costume* looks all right, then I look dead and it's too darn late to look all right."

I had no clue what she was on about so I shuffled some papers and ignored her. Liz was used to that. By the time I left the campus at the end of the day, I still hadn't seen any ghosts, goblins, Frankensteins or otherwise. I crossed Sherbrooke Street against the red light—unheard of! You could fire a cannon down de Maisonneuve and not hit a soul. The streets were empty, empty, empty. This was the

Halloween that Quebec forgot. Quebecers had something else on their minds. This was Referendum Day. Everyone was home, watching CBC.

The repercussions of the vote and Jacques Parizeau's words profoundly shook Quebecers that night. They forged new attitudes and new intolerances. A week is a long time in politics, but *je me souviens* has a special meaning here.

A year or so later, interest rates were low enough that Tony and I considered the benefits of home ownership.

"Not in Quebec!" he said firmly. "I'm not doing the referendum thing again. I've done it twice now. I don't want to live with this kind of instability any more."

"Okay," I replied. "Where to next then, Batman?"

"Ontario."

His answer surprised me into silence.

As I trawled the Internet for properties across the invisible divide, I came across an affordable few in the Ingleside area. Although conveniently close to Highway 401 for easy access to Montreal, Ottawa and Kingston, Ingleside is still far enough away from anything to be labelled the boonies. Hence the price.

"We used to go camping in that area when we were kids," said Tony. "It used to rain from the moment we arrived to the moment we left. It's not magnificent or anything, but it's quite pretty. Lots of islands, parkways, sleepy farmhouses, wildlife, beautiful river banks—it's right on the St. Lawrence Seaway, you know. Some old villages were drowned when the Seaway and power dam were created. I think you can still see their remains and the old streets if you go diving around the Long Sault Parkway. Bit spooky really. Other than that, it's as flat as a clean piece of paper, with good roads to boot. Sure—I could live there."

"That's all very well, but what do people do for a living?" I said, thinking in more practical terms. The closest town of any consequence was Cornwall, thirty kilometres away, set on its own beautiful waterfront. Both wealthy and neglected at the same time, Cornwall suffered from, yet was also saved by, its proximity to Montreal, Ottawa and Kingston. Tony might find a job there, but I would be hard-pressed.

"We'll think of something. We're clever," he replied.

I didn't doubt that, so I cast my mind to work on potential rural revenue streams for a salesman and a pencil-pusher.

"Eureka!" I shouted several days later.

"What? What's wrong?" asked Tony, completely forgetting my little project.

"We're going to leave the rat-race behind. I have the perfect plan. All we need to do is spend some time studying commercial organic market gardening."

"That's good," he replied. "Cuz I, for one, know nothing about it."

I had persuaded Tony to go vegetarian a few years before. Never big meat-eaters, we were down to the odd chicken breast (which I gingerly handled with a knife and fork because the thought of touching raw flesh and goose-bumpy skin made my own skin crawl) and ground beef in pasta sauces. After discovering that organic produce tasted so much better and was in keeping with our environmental values, there was no going back. A few dreadful failures during the learning curve aside, I became adept at producing tasty vegetarian meals and Tony readily adapted to the sheer volume of food he could consume without putting on weight.

"Well, think about it," I said. "Organic vegetables are highly sought-after. We buy them ourselves so we know what they sell for. We wouldn't need endless acres of land to make a reasonable living. We can sell directly to the consumer and, best of all, we don't need a ton of machinery either."

"Plus, whatever we don't sell, we can eat or freeze!" added Tony, getting excited.

This idea was a winner. It turned into a plan, then into reality. And that's how we became statistics in the Second Great Exodus.

the house that jack built

Never buy a house in the deep of a Canadian winter. We did, and now we know why other people don't.

As we rounded the bend on Knox Road, our first impression of the farm was "cute." Run down, but cute. A hundred and fifty-year old post-and-beam homestead on eighty-five unkempt acres. Unlike others in the neighbourhood still bearing the original clapboard that needs to be sanded and painted every five years, this one had been modernized with white aluminum siding. In spite of that, it had retained its old-world charm and rural appeal, in part because of the gnarly apple tree and the must-have lilacs in the yard, and the rusty tin roof. I felt drawn to its welcome and the simplicity of its structure.

A monstrous set of gleaming white—and very sharp-looking—teeth, bad breath and beady black eyes surrounded by a vast rug of black fur greeted us at the porch.

"It's all right," gulped Moynahan, the real-estate agent. "He's not usually like this. He knows me. I'm trying to remember his name…"

Nobody wanted to test how deep those teeth could sink into our ankles, and in the owners' absence, we contented ourselves with a look-see around the yard. A walk around the brushy fields would have been both wise and useful, but we deemed it unsafe. This was 1998, the winter of the infamous ice storm. Whatever damage might have occurred in this neck of the woods lay blanketed in snow. Nothing was out there but a blinding whiteness from which city folk wearing city boots would never emerge intact.

"You gonna be there this time?" Moynahan lectured the Chartrands about our next appointment. "You can't sell a house with a snarling dog on the porch if you're not gonna be there."

Cub was lollygagging on his back when we arrived. He sat up, yawned widely and let his tongue hang loose in greeting.

"Cub?" I whispered to Tony. "They've got to be joking. Wolf in sheep's clothing, more like." The three of us tiptoed past him.

"You'll see that a lot of renovation has already been done," Moynahan started his sales pitch. He waved his arms expansively, smiling.

The inside was interesting to say the least. It had indeed been renovated extensively—if not always logically. We couldn't figure out the advantage in moving the downstairs toilet from the laundry room (the diverted piping in the basement was incriminating evidence) into a cubbyhole in the *dining* room. But there was incredible potential. The ground floor had high, bevelled baseboards; the doors, set in wide oak frames, were solid pine with original fixtures; where the floor was exposed we could see thick, pine boards; and the large windows were framed from floor to ceiling in oak. This was a house made from original growth forest. We were sold.

"You want to grow vegetables? This is the ideal place," said the Chartrands, correctly taking us for the fools we were. "We eat out of our garden all year." Come spring, I found the garden—measuring the surface area of a tablecloth in the lowest, most frost-prone area of the yard—so I think not!

Without the benefit of hindsight, however, idyllic thoughts percolated into the danger zone of our minds. After a lightning visit, we placed an offer conditional on financing and a sound inspection.

In a similar lightning visit on his way to spend the afternoon with his brother in Cornwall, the home inspector pronounced the place "in excellent shape for its age." It never occurred to us that this might be a caveat in disguise. There's no other way a qualified man could miss the insane wiring, the bizarre plumbing, the leaky foundation—and he didn't even go up onto the roof. His excuse was it might be icy. It wouldn't be a problem if he were properly equipped to attach himself to the chimney. And then he wouldn't have missed the huge gaps in the overlapping tin and the lack of insulation up there, would he now?

My very first shower was rendered memorable when the hot water faucet came off in my hand and the drain blocked, leaving me naked, soapy and with an urgent problem to solve. We discovered that the old aluminum windows leaked like sieves; the basement radiated such dampness that no paper in the house stayed crisp; the fields and woods are full of generations of garbage; and, had we been able to look under all that snow, we would have known that that the ice-storm did as much damage here as it did in Quebec.

"On the up-side," said Tony, one day, looking up from the array of tools he had neatly spread out for his latest project. "By the time we're done putting our mark on the joint, it'll be exactly the homestead we were looking for in the first place."

meet the cast

Let me introduce you to the colourful people who make up our *entourage*.

Me, I was born and raised in England by a French mother and a Mauritian father. I was bilingual almost before I could walk. Along with my peers, I did the daily commute from the 'burbs to central London, drove my desk for seven hours and then did the same commute in reverse. I loved the hustle and bustle of the big city—the theatre, rock concerts, art galleries. The day I fell asleep on a fellow commuter's shoulder, lulled by the rhythmic rocking of the train, I knew there had to be more to life…

I arrived in Canada at age twenty-three, expecting to stay a year in Montreal and work my way home through the Eastern Seaboard, Cuba, the Bahamas, etc. But the working papers I had diligently completed turned out to be immigration papers. Back then, Canada was an open door so it's the government's fault I'm still here. By today's standards, the four hundred dollars in my pocket and two bulging suitcases would never qualify me. I decided it didn't change the game plan. What did was meeting Tony within three weeks of my arrival. I still haven't seen the Eastern Seaboard, Cuba, the Bahamas, etc.

Tony is a practical man and extremely clever with his hands. It's his manifestation of the huge artistic talent running in the family. He's also a perfectionist, which you cannot be when renovating an ancient and crumbling house. It has caused much agony and blasphemy. Always game to add some zest into his life, this man is not afraid to experiment with plumbing and electricity—preferably not at the same time. His sisters still live in Montreal. Susie is a regular visitor and we can always count on her to pitch in with our crazy projects and add a few ideas of her own.

Domtar is our neighbour on the west and north side. The company owns enormous tracts of bush in the area that it manages for its paper mill in Cornwall. It seems uninterested in the land beside us and I'm hoping it's been forgotten. It would be a shame to lose the trees and habitat to logging. Its conspicuous absence makes Domtar the best possible neighbour.

Roger and Mary Chisholm are on our east side. They have a two-acre chunk taken out of our southeast field and sold to them by George Vanderveen who, at the time, owned our house and land as well as the barn and fifty-five acres across the road—the full, original homestead. Roger grew up in our house, and I guess he just wanted to come home. His father was the last to actually farm our acres and, back then, it was by horse, not tractor. It's a bit bizarre wondering what memories he has of the house in his youth, but he's a wealth of local information and a good neighbour. We don't see much of Mary—the odd over-the-fence conversation in summer, or from a distance when hanging the laundry.

East of them were the Hennessys. John has piercing blue eyes and shaves his head but keeps a ZZ-Top beard.

The first words he uttered to me were, "Do you speak English?" I don't think I look *that* foreign. He'd spotted the Quebec plates on our car so I suppose it was a legitimate question. His wife, Julie, is a grand pastry cook (she used to exchange pies for Tony's cookies) and excellent homemaker. They moved to Cornwall in 2000, citing a lack of local activities and friends for their three daughters.

The Hennessys were replaced by Steve and Ruth Cantley. At last, a couple in our age-group. We were getting quite worried. They're very nice, have endless big-boy toys and seem to be very well plugged in to local events thanks to a whole slew of relatives in the community.

Across the road from them were Doug and Sue Winter. They're an older couple: he's British, she's Danish. We had some horrible misunderstanding with them about cats and we don't talk much anymore. They, too, eventually moved closer to modern amenities.

A few months after we moved in, the barn and land across the road from us were sold to Matt Farstead, his father and an endless assortment of family and friends. To put it politely, the barn could be described as weather-beaten. In our less patient moments, we call it an eyesore. Either way, it has certainly seen better days. It is, however, fully equipped for a large workshop in one corner and has at least eight horse stalls along with a gigantic area for hay storage and a whole upper floor. Matt keeps/boards/breeds horses. We haven't figured out which. It's a recipe for trouble since there's no house on that side and, therefore, nobody on-site to supervise them.

Dan Flansbury lives in the next township, but as the dodo flies, just a few fields diagonally behind us. His wife,

Katrina, works brutal hours in Ottawa. I didn't see their son, Sean, in clothes until he was two years old. Katrina had given up keeping him clean and out of trouble on the farm so he spent his early childhood in his birthday suit. Definitely his father's son. On the other hand, their daughter, Lianne, is a responsible little girl and eager to please. We found them through the auspices of Tom Maynard of Country Lane Organics whom we met at the Newington county fair. We were looking for someone to revitalize, work and generally keep nature at bay in three of our four fields. Katrina and I became firm friends. There ain't a secret we don't share—Tony and Dan being prime fodder for our gossip.

Joan Alexander. Dearest friend and cat-lady. I have rarely met a more intelligent, independent, opinionated, passionate person in my life. She was kind (or foolhardy) enough to allow us to pursue our dream by letting me lodge in her home in Montreal during the early years when I still worked at McGill.
Other eclectic people drift in and out of our lives from time to time. You'll meet them, too.

the hare-brained plans of mice and (wo)men

At one stage or another, most of us dream of the simple life; a log cabin, a wood-stove, a garden full of vegetables, an Adirondack chair from which to admire loons on a still lake. What could be more serene? What could be more removed from the blistering pace of the cities into which so many of us are crammed? And yet, who wouldn't go stark raving nuts if left in those idyllic surroundings for very long? There's no cinema, pharmacy or convenience store round the corner; no cable TV; nowhere to go on a Saturday night. You just have to get used to the ho-hum slow pace of country life and the dearth of amenities that urbanites take for granted. Or move back to the city.

"That's it! We're done with the city and its crazy values. We have everything we need right here. We're "back-to-the-landers" now," Tony and I cried in unison. Giddy with delight that we had literally, not figuratively, "bought the farm," we were determined to run it as such. We yearned to sit on that Adirondack chair in the evening sun.

But before our wonderful idea could prosper into a tangible reality, we had to jump some hurdles. Financial and knowledge-based hurdles. We hit the books in a serious way over the winter. I read everything the library had to offer on

14

vegetable growing, soil management and compost. Tony pored over home renovation manuals until he could stand it no longer. *This Old House* had nothing on him.

Our financial plan perfectly matched our ability to fight the current. I would keep my job at McGill for a couple of years as a source of regular income until we stood on our own two agricultural feet. To avoid a four-hour daily commute—a sure road to insanity—Tony drove me to Montreal on Monday mornings and back out on Friday evenings, and thus we launched the long-distance phase of our relationship. I stayed with Joan Alexander during the week where I discovered that her entire culinary repertoire can be written on the back of a postage stamp with space left over, and that it *is* possible to have too many cats. So I became chief cook and washer-upper and—when she worked away from home—auntie to the cats.

In the meantime, Tony applied his considerable talents and new-found knowledge to house renovation in winter, to yard renovation, cleaning up fence-lines and clearing brush, dead farm junk and boulders from the fields in spring and autumn. In summer, we worked the vegetable garden together, organically, in harmony with Mother Nature, the changing seasons and the wildlife around us.

Farm profits—an oxymoron if ever there was one—were earmarked for further home improvements and/or indispensable agricultural hardware. With a crescendo of demand in the community-supported agriculture model of organic vegetable farming we proposed to follow, we anticipated enough financial security to live off our, albeit small, farm income within a few years.

Naïveté can be so charming.

a woman's kitchen is her castle

Two rooms away, Tony heard me muttering under my breath.

"What's wrong?" he called.

"You wanna know? Here's what!" I redirected my irritation at him.

"That's your dinner, right there," I said, pointing to the litre of ginger-carrot soup I had just spilled onto the worn, brown kitchen carpet. I was more concerned at the waste of perfectly good soup than the addition of another stain.

"This kitchen is revolting. We have to do something about it—now!" I added, waving a soupy rag in the air.

The kitchen is a one-and-a-half storey add-on to the original house that has been "improved" many times. Whenever he visits, Roger refers to it as the East Kitchen, confirming that it was already there in his youth, but not in which configuration. By the time the house fell into our hands, the floor of the upper storey had been mostly removed, leaving a small loft-like space at one end, stairs to the upper floor at the other end and an extremely high vaulted ceiling surfaced in chipboard. Some handyman had thought it clever to put drywall on the lower part of the walls, chipboard panelling above that and disguise the lot with beige wallpaper. The beige melamine countertop was cracked and burnt, and the oak cupboard doors were darkly stained—perfect for masking those grubby fingerprints. The dim light fixture hung so low we had to walk around it, and brown curtains covered the windows. Overwhelmingly, the effect was dark, glum and brown, brown, brown.

The curtains bit the dust in the first week. Partly because I had knocked my head enough times on that cursed light fixture that I wanted to rip it out and partly because our desire/need for maximum sunlight to replace said fixture overcame our scant regard for privacy. The detour any peeping toms had to make to watch two people having dinner in a small house on an unpaved country road would be deterrent enough.

"Okay," said Tony, taking a look around. The moving crates were barely unpacked and already I was hatching projects for him. Neither of us had ever tackled a reno this big. The thought was daunting. In fact, it daunted us into major procrastination, but the final blow came unexpectedly.

Because the only artificial light came from the not-yet-ripped-out fixture in the middle of the room, the counters were always obscured by our shadows. One sliced finger and much blood and bandages later, Tony bought a row of three adjustable halogens to fix onto the ceiling below the loft, over the counters. Properly adjusted, these would solve all our lighting issues.

"You're not going to believe this," I heard from the loft where he had just torn up the floorboards. "I have to rewire the whole kitchen just to install this one little thing. Talk about one step forward, two steps back."

He straightened up to show me a fistful of spaghetti-like wires, some chewed by mice, dating back to the early days of electricity. In so doing, he caught his jeans on a nail, lost his already precarious balance—stepping carefully as he was on the narrow beams—and came crashing through the loft ceiling, landing squarely in the sink.

"Are you hurt?" I asked, flooded by a wave of guilt that this was my fault and we should have left that stupid fixture in after all.

"My pride and my butt—in that order," he replied tightly, still clutching the wires. Tony is a man of few words.

There was no turning back now. A flurry of activity transformed the kitchen into a skeleton of its former self. The pile of debris we removed took two days to burn. Natural light poured in. It was very heartening.

I can't bear to dwell on the difficulties we had, or the lessons we learned the hard way. Suffice to say, a house this old has many idiosyncrasies. The illogical wiring, for a start. The upper and lower walls not being quite vertical, so that after the drywall went in on the upper level, we had to build the join out with many, many buckets of mud. The lack of right angles. As luck would have it, the corner for the perfect, new, L-shaped counter was greater than ninety degrees so instead of having to chip into the wall, Tony added a wedge behind one end of the counter and adjusted the cabinets underneath accordingly. The undulating floor. Levelling was a mean task and one at which we didn't entirely succeed. The checkerboard tiles we chose served only to highlight the ripples. The cathedral ceiling. While I laboured over a hot keyboard at McGill, Tony laboured on a hinged ladder clinging impossibly to narrow beams, screwdriver clenched between his teeth, fistful of screws in one hand, weighty sheet of drywall slithering down the wall in the other. This he told me over the phone, after the fact. No regard for safety or common sense, that man!

By the end of the three-month project, the novelty of doing dishes on our knees in the bathtub had more than worn off. So had wheeling the stove back to the outlet every meal time, using a plank set on two chairs as a make-shift counter and not being able to find the cereal in the morning because it was under one of many dustsheets.

The result, however, is a visual delight. The kitchen is now pale blue and white with pine trim, wainscotting and stairs. Sunlight floods in and reflects off the walls and, yes, the new light fixture is at a reasonable height.

That first winter, we discovered that the kitchen was still inadequately insulated. Cold air poured in through the electrical outlets and sat at body height because, as we were reminded daily, warm air supplied by the furnace rose straight into that wonderful cathedral ceiling where it hung uselessly. We barely needed a fridge at all. "There can't be many other people with inner soles in their slippers to keep out the cold floor," I found myself thinking. The following spring, I noticed that the counter was coming away from the wall. At the same time, the porch door refused to close, as if the frame were no longer square.

"Y'know," cursed Tony, thinking of the damp basement. "This house is probably built on a swamp. It's destined to be in perpetual motion."

When the St. Lawrence River was dammed in 1958 to form the Seaway and the islands, thousands of acres of good farmland suddenly became thousands of acres of new swamps, marshes and shallows. Also built in the name of progress, Highway 401 and the VIA train line run parallel to the Seaway blocking the natural drainage to the river and creating an equal number of swamps, marshes and shallows on the other side. Already a low-lying, clay area with little topsoil when the house and many of its contemporaries were built, these new installations hadn't helped any. Tony wasn't far from the truth; we just didn't know it yet.

"Sweetie," I replied, looking at a brand new crack meandering its way above the back door towards the ceiling. "This house has been here for a hundred and fifty years. It'll still be here long after we're gone. *Après moi, le déluge.*"

I was relieved, if somewhat perplexed, that everything fell back into place after the spring thaw—and every year after that.

One day in the very distant future and when we have nothing better to do, we'll do what our predecessors did—renovate the renovation. At least this time, we know the pitfalls.

dirt in our fingernails, farming in our blood

Community-Supported Agriculture (CSA) looked like a blessing in disguise.

Here's how it works. Customers, called sharers, buy a share of the vegetable harvest at a pre-established price at the beginning of the season. This gives the farmer the necessary capital to buy seed, supplies and other necessities, without having to go cap in hand to the bank. In return, the sharer receives weekly baskets—his *share*—of produce according to what's in season and what's ready for harvest, quantity regardless. We didn't want to bother fixing weekly prices for vegetables, or deal with possible unsold surpluses. This seemed tailor-made for us.

"Why are there no tomatoes this week?" a sharer asked me at the beginning of the season.

Apparently, our brochure was not crystal clear or expectations were unreasonable.

"Because this is April in Eastern Ontario, and I can't give you tomatoes at earth-bound prices without a greenhouse," I felt like saying.

"Because you are supporting *local* agriculture. And right now, peas, salad greens, rhubarb and spinach are in season," was my diplomatic response. "It's not quite the same as shopping at Loblaws."

"Uh." The disappointment was audible.

"Don't worry. By the end of the season, you'll have had a good variety of veggies. But remember that everything has its time."

"Uh."

CSA encourages sharers to learn where their food comes from and how it gets to their doorstep in the form of working visits to "their" farm. Our offer of a substantial rebate, a maximum of three times, to any sharer who wanted to work for the day should have been irresistible. Many promised faithfully to be there whenever we needed them. Come summer, only one family showed up.

"When would you need us?" asked Monique Gauthier, earnestly reaching for her diary as I signed her up. "We want to experience everything."

Their first date was in late May. Spring had sprung wet and the southeast field looked like a construction site after a monsoon. It was our first year, so we were working with a blank canvas. The thought of two extra bodies to help out was a great relief.

"Spades, forks, garden-claw, hoe," said Tony, wielding an armful of hardware. "We need to dig twenty-four raised beds, nine by one metre each. We'll take soil from what will be the pathways, pile it onto what will be the beds and then work the beds so they're ready to plant. Perfect to build up an appetite. Shame it's a little muddy out there."

Monique and her partner, Patrick, looked nervous. She mumbled something about her sciatica and her manicure. To their credit, however, they worked stoically, doggedly and without complaining about the mosquitoes or the mud. Between the four of us, we got the job done.

Monique straightened up slowly, using the spade-handle for leverage. The blisters on her hands matched what remained of her vermillion nail polish and the veins in her temples were taut enough to snap. She looked more dishevelled than when she arrived and her smile had paled somewhat.

"What do people around here do for fun?" she asked wanly.

"Ice cream in Morrisburg by the river," I suggested.

The smile re-appeared. Ice cream will do that.

To Clara, their daughter, I gave a job I thought would delight any youngster—an opportunity to get grubby. Well, sticky, really.

"This is called tanglefoot," I told her, holding out a tube of something akin to glue. "It's a sticky natural resin that we use to trap flies on these fake fruit hanging from the apple and cherry trees. That way, they don't lay their eggs in the real fruit."

Within a short time, she appeared dejectedly at my side. To my consternation, I saw that she had distributed an even film up to her elbows and in her hair. We spent the next little while trying to remove this stuff from her person without resorting to sandpaper or scissors and, especially, without her mother seeing. Who knew it doesn't come off with water or alcohol!

We paid them for the day. In view of what they/we had accomplished, it was a pittance. Slave labour. I believe they took back with them to Montreal a whole new appreciation for the work involved in food production. They cancelled their remaining dates.

So far, CSA looked great. The flip side, however, came every week when it was time to prepare the baskets for delivery. Instead of dressing in our Sunday best, we wore our Sunday rags to pick, cut, wash, trim, sort and divide the harvest into equal shares, bag it, spritz the bags for moisture, make sure those sharers who had been on vacation received a catch-up share and record who got what. The administration was mind-blowing. I was already doing enough paperwork at McGill that I didn't want to do more on the weekends when I was supposed to be *farming!*

"We can't give people wet lettuce," said Tony one Sunday, bringing six milk crates of tender salad greens out of a torrential downpour "It'll rot before they get it home."

"Well, we can't do all this in the salad spinner either," I replied. "Not if we want to go to bed tonight at all."

Do we have a choice?" he countered sourly, reaching for the spinner.

"Okay," I replied, beaten. "I'll sort. You spin."

One hour and only one milk-crate later, this method was proving as useless as I had predicted. Tony had an illumination.

"We'll use the rinse and gentle spin cycle in the washing machine."

My eyes opened wide.

"Oh yeah? And what about the wildlife?" Our lettuce was always inhabited.

"Too bad about the wildlife."

We emptied three milk crates of salad greens into our brand new washing machine, set it for ten minutes, screwed our eyes shut and waited for it to clog.

"Oooh," I said, opening the lid when the cycle was over. "We should have thought of this ages ago. The lettuce looks great. What a time-saver! And you know what…?" my voice echoed from the depths of the drum. "It even separates the slugs out." I reached farther down and captured some very dizzy slugs trying their best to get outta there.

The combination of wet weekend and lettuce season didn't happen again that year, so our new-found time never materialized either.

Most of the baskets came with me to McGill, where I crammed them into two small fridges, to the detriment of my colleagues' lunches. The other baskets spent the day in coolers on Joan Alexander's front porch, where they would wait… and wait… and wait…

"Monday is the established day for pick up," I'd say to a sharer over the phone, a day or so later. "Your fresh, organic and not entirely cheap veggies are wasting away in a cooler."

Threats and entreaties made no difference. Sharers showed up at any hour, any day of the week and took away some produce that would doubtless go straight from the basket to the trash. I hated to see such waste.

The following year, I rewrote the brochure and further explained the vagaries of the system to every sharer who signed up. Our goal was to get a group of dedicated, hard core, anti-GMO health-freaks. It worked. They thought we were gods and ate—almost literally—out of our hands.

Whoever said extremists are a bad thing?

the grass is greener, better, shorter on the other side

Everybody loves a good lawn. I can understand the aesthetics of that. But I'm not sure why people with two acres to mow—that is, anybody in the country would a) want to mow that much and b) care so deeply if there's a weed or two in it. These are not the miniscule city lawns that can be trimmed in half an hour with a pair of nail clippers.

In our search for cheap soaker hose for the vegetable garden, we became familiar with the horticultural section of many a chain store.

"Check this out," gasped Tony, at our first stop.

He was standing in an aisle stocked, pharmacy-like, with an overwhelming array of fungicides, herbicides, pesticides and plant-specific, trifid-making nutrients. As lowly apartment-dwellers in Montreal, we never had reason to visit these aisles. A whole new world was opening up.

"Yeah, hun," I replied. "But I bet you can't find more than two that don't carry a skull and crossbones somewhere near the small print. We're supposed to be certified organic, remember."

"Oh." He stepped back, as if poisoned by mere proximity.

The hose temporarily forgotten, we did a search-and-compare against our list of permitted products—and came up with rotenone and Safer's Soap. Two items total—and rotenone is only permitted under controlled circumstances.

"No wonder everybody else's grass looks so good," he muttered. "It's on steroids."

Walking through the watering equipment, the rotating sprinklers, sprinkler pipes, ordinary hose pipes, hose reels, hose connectors, watering cans, spray heads—need I go on?—I began to feel both comfort in living in a country with so much fresh water and confusion about the way it is applied.

"Amazing, isn't it? People spend all this money to water their lawn, fertilize it, nurture it, all to help it grow—and the minute it does, they're right out there mowing it down."

"Roger and Doug Winter certainly are," replied Tony. "You'd think there are more interesting things to do in retirement than sitting on a small tractor going round in circles every four or five days."

Back home, we examined our lawn. It needed to be rolled badly. A large percentage had been aggressively colonized by moss, a low-growing, creeping weed with the prettiest blue flowers in spring and dandelions. If we wanted to get rid of these "weeds" in favour of the grass, it would be a mammoth task.

"I'm not spending my precious weekends pulling dandelions up by hand," I said testily. "It's thankless and pointless. In fact, we should be encouraging this creeping weed-thing to suffocate the grass. It doesn't grow tall and it doesn't need mowing. I don't really care what the lawn is made up of as long as it's green."

"Well, then we really should have watered it, cuz right now, if you look around, there are plenty of brown patches where it's been scorched by the sun." I hate it when Tony has a point.

"You want to spend your time watering a lawn when there's a thirsty vegetable garden nearby?—something that actually returns cash for your effort. Besides," I added, glancing over at Roger's lush green carpet. "It'll recover in the autumn and grow gangbusters in the spring."

Tony drew the short straw and the mowing fell mostly to him. Our parents had tortured neither one of us into garden chores—we didn't know what lay ahead.

Our available cash flow limited the first major yard purchase to an antique push-mower. It was excruciating, exhausting, boring! There aren't enough adjectives to cover the range of sensations flowing through our minds and bodies. We acknowledged defeat with a loan and bought a second-hand riding-mower. In his haste to finish this chore in under two hours, Tony drives it like a Formula One car. It can turn corners on two wheels although I doubt it was designed to. Every now and again, he forgets about low-hanging branches and avoids decapitation by a whisker.

Over the winter, I had one of my Eureka! moments.

"We need sheep. They don't forage quite as much as goats. We could get rid of the mower and save a ton of time, gas and energy. What could be better?"

"No!" the reply was firm. The war was lost before it was begun.

Meanwhile, spring is coming and the grass is getting greener… and longer…

drive-in or drive-by

England doesn't have drive-in movie theatres. I suppose the population density makes land too valuable for such frivolous use, and when I was young, we didn't have liberal access to cars.

My friends and I knew what they were. We had all seen *Grease* and knew the song, *Stranded at the Drive-In*, by heart. John Travolta was the heart-throb of my pre-pubescent generation and I still love that film. But I had never been to one. Yet here in Ingleside, only eight kilometres from home, in all its glory, was a drive-in theatre. We *had* to go! The reason there's a drive-in theatre in a village of, oh, perhaps two thousand souls, is the camping boom of the Sixties and Seventies in the area. The Long Sault Parkway, its series of quaint little islands and beaches in the St. Lawrence River connected by causeways, and the opportunity for a bit of quiet fishing, canoeing or bird-watching, was the perfect destination spot for city-worn vacationers. With the passage of time, the advent of RVs and the affordability of rental cottages, an unstoppable decline in the industry began in the Eighties and continues today.

"We can't go yet," Tony told me soon after my discovery. "At this latitude, they only operate in the peak of summer for the tourists. When we camped here as kids, it served as one of our drying-out trips after it rained. That and touring the power station in Cornwall. Maybe my parents thought they could nuke us dry." I remembered that his childhood camping vacations were non-stop rain so they must have gone a lot. I waited semi-patiently until the summer solstice and then could stand it no longer.

"What's showing and when?" I eagerly asked the person on the other end of the line.

There were three films, two of them first run and a third one for children, for only eight dollars.

"And what is the start time?" I asked.

"Half an hour after sundown."

I hadn't counted on this. It was late June, the days were at their longest and I'm not known for my ability to keep my eyes open beyond eleven o'clock! It didn't bode well.

"Well, at least we're here before the crowds," I said, as we settled into our chosen spot. We were almost the first to arrive. Tony headed for the concession stand for his post-dinner snack. He returned with an armful of soda and nachos.

"I might have gone for the hot dogs for old times' sake," he said. "But the smell put me off. Funny how things change."

A quarter to ten rolled around and the first film started. A cartoon. A cartoon, for crying out loud! Who in the world is old enough to still be awake and want to watch a cartoon at the flicks at ten o'clock? And not just one, either. This was an endless series of mindless, modern animation.

"If this goes on for an hour, and is followed by two films of approximately two hours each… we'll still be here at dawn!" Never mind the eight bucks. How on earth was I going to stay awake? More to the point, why hadn't I thought of asking about this when I called?

We didn't see much of those cartoons. Three adults (Tony's sister, Susie, was staying with us that weekend) stuffed into the tiny Mazda and breathing adult-sized breath were creating heavy condensation on the windows. We were effectively boxed in. No amount of wiping could clear the windshield. We opened the windows, let in a swarm of mosquitoes, promptly wound the windows back up again and spent the next cozy few minutes ridding ourselves of the intruders.

The first of the real films started at about eleven thirty. I wiped the windows—again—and looked around. Of the dozen or so cars whose inhabitants had suffered through the cartoons, a good half were leaving.

"Their windows are perfectly clear," said Susie, still wiping ours. "What's wrong with these people? The good stuff starts now. And why aren't there more people here, anyway?"

We hunkered down in our seats, pretending to be invisible to the gnats and trying hard not to breathe. It was warm and dark and I was asleep in minutes. Tony woke me up at some ungodly hour—back home. Apparently, the two films had been quite good.

The drive-in closed permanently at the end of that summer. They couldn't make a go of it. A great shame. Nowadays, the campers mostly come in motor homes bristling with satellite dishes and antennas. They don't feel the need for this great North American institution that flavoured so many films and became a rite of passage for a generation. I'm glad I went before it died.

the inspector cometh

"The inspector's coming. The inspector's coming."

Dan Flansbury was in a panic. Organic certification agencies are omnipotent; the rules complicated and plentiful; and the inspectors wield the power of business or bust. Because our other fields fell under his tender ministrations, Dan's certification also covered Harvest Moon Farm.

"What? Right now?" replied Tony, over the phone. He was still in his pyjamas.

"No," said Dan. "Tomorrow!"

Katrina, Dan's long-suffering wife, once told me that his university education and the frequent curve balls life threw at him simply washed over him like water off a duck's back. This didn't sound like a man who would panic at the thought of a certification inspector. Where his farm was concerned, however, Dan was finding new and improved ways of fighting the tide. His general sang-froid no longer applied.

"Got-things-to-do-See-you-tomorrow-Bye." Tony was left, phone in hand, nonplussed.

Essentially, certification is proof that the land, seed, crop growing methods and animal husbandry all meet a documented standard. For instance, because our fields had been neglected (or, in farm parlance, left fallow) for well over ten years, Dan was able to claim them as organic immediately and avoid the carefully-monitored transition phase.

Good soil (nurtured by crop rotation, green manures, compost and natural fertilizers) is the product of time and careful management, says the book. To that prim statement, Tony and I will add that it is also the product of much sweat, labour and occasional heat stroke.

To make that good soil, we needed a truckful of equally good compost. After raking the leaves from the yard into a pile and adding the droppings and bedding straw from the chickens who came to live with us in spring, we were still well short.

"Where can we get tons of leaves without doing much work…?" I mused.

The answer came to me in the middle of the night. That's when I do my best thinking. I refrained from waking Tony.

"Sweetie," I said, over breakfast the next morning. "I know how to solve our leaf issue."

Tony looked at me as though he knew I was about to say something daft.

"We can drive around the village under cover of darkness and take those orange leaf bags with Halloween faces on them."

"You want to steal people's Halloween?" he said incredulously.

I wasn't sure if he was upset at that or at the thought of driving through Ingleside with a trunk full of leaves. My idea wasn't going well. I needed a Plan B.

"Sweetie," I repeated, over breakfast another morning. "I know how to solve our leaf issue."

Tony wasn't waiting with bated breath to hear this one.

"We can get them from Upper Canada Village. You know, that spot by the memorial. All we have to do is bag 'em and bring 'em back."

In a perfect location overlooking the Seaway that led to its creation, Upper Canada Village is the new home to many of the historic homes, buildings and businesses rescued from the floodwaters. Recreating rural and small town life in the late nineteenth century, it's educational, fun and refreshing. Right next to it is the memorial to the Battle of Crysler's Farm, scene of an unsuccessful American attempt to invade Canada during the war of 1812 and, in more modern times, natural collection point for all of the park's fallen leaves.

This plan still involved a trunkful of leaves, so I wasn't sure he'd go for it. Let's just say he couldn't think of a better idea in time.

So that's how we found ourselves one Saturday morning of total autumn downpour, loading garbage bags of soggy leaves into the car, the trunk and the trailer, and trying very hard not to look conspicuous as local and late-season tourists drove by wondering what these two idiots were playing at. In his canary-yellow rainsuit, Tony looked like a long, lean cob of corn. In hot pink and black, I looked no less unusual.

"You know what?" he said, rain running down the end of his nose. "This might make great compost, but it's a helluva lot easier to toss a bunch of chemical fertilizers into the soil and get the same results."

He was missing the point, but I too had felt that burning desire for chemical solutions the day I discovered that an infestation of Colorado Potato Beetles had eaten our eggplant plants down to the stalks.

"Prevention is key," said Dan, in response to my question.

"Skip the lecture, Dan," I interrupted. "I need a solution—quick!"

"You'll have to squish them individually for about ten days. By then, you'll have broken the cycle."

"You want me to squish bugs with my fingers?" I said. "I think not!"

Dan nodded. He could barely contain his smile. City girl, he thought. Now, I know Dan grew up in deepest Toronto. He and Katrina bought their place only a few years before we arrived. In the hope of getting a better solution to my problem, I chose to ignore that crooked grin instead of wiping it off his face.

"Isn't there something I can use? Something organic I can spray?" I continued in desperation. I did *not* want to have to do this.

Dan shook his head, still smiling.

The bright red larvae are so juicy that, even with gloves, the process disgusted me. I started using garden scissors to chop them in half. Ever keen to find short"cuts"—no pun intended—Tony came up with a better solution.

"Whatever are you doing?" I asked, seeing him join length after length of electrical extension cord.

"Wait and see," he replied.

He brought out the shop-vac.

"You're not really..." I started.

"You bet," he said, nonetheless looking around to see if anybody might be watching.

I wish I'd had a camera. Tony and the shop vac took care of the eggplant and potato plants in a jiffy.

"There," he said, vacuum hose in one hand, earplugs in the other. "All done."

He was right. Not a beetle or larva in sight. And it certainly beat getting a squirt of red bug juice in the eye.

Having lived through some intensely unpleasant moments for the sake of our ideals and followed the agency's rulebook to the letter, we pooh-poohed Dan's fears about "the visit."

The inspector spent most of the day with Dan. By the time they reached us, he was a little twitchy. There was a certain tension in the air.

"I need letters from your seed suppliers confirming that your purchases are non-GMO and one from your neighbour stating that no chemicals were used on these fields before you took them over. I can't issue your certification without these documents," she said dryly.

Tony was immediately flustered.

"Uhhh… okay," he said. "I can get those."

"I also need to see your bills for chicken feed, seed and anything else you bought."

"Uhh… well. We didn't keep them," Tony gulped. "But Tom Maynard at Country Lane Organics, our feed supplier, knows us. He'll vouch, I'm sure."

She looked mighty displeased.

"Okay. We'll measure your coop now and then look at the fields."

Tony thanked the stars the coop had just been cleaned as she carefully measured to check the ratio of floor space to bird. The three of them moved on to a hands-and-knees inspection of the vegetable beds, checking for soil composition and possible granules of illicit fertilizer. She swung by the tool shed and did an impromptu examination for traces of powders and containers of forbidden products. Then she was gone.

I wasn't there, but rumour has it that both guys were sweating when she left.

Dan begged me to send the documents quickly so he could get his certificate. I got them out to her within three days of her visit.

Several months later, the Executive Director of Organic Crop Producers and Processors (the certification body) called.

"We need some documents to complete your file," he began.

"What?" I replied. "What other document could you possibly want?"

"We need letters from your seed sources indicating that your purchases meet our standards, and a letter from your neighbour saying that your land was unfertilized and unused for more than three years."

"You have all of those already."

"Oh no we don't."

"Oh yes you do." I have a talent for attracting circular conversations. "I faxed them to your inspector almost immediately after her visit."

Looks like the guys sweated for nothing.

alarm bells in our heads

The countryside is probably the safest place to live in Canada. Not because of the low crime rate. Not because it's sparsely populated. And certainly not because it's well policed. But because country homes are replete with dogs armed with fearsome gnashers and big, big barks. An effective deterrent.

"Oh, you don't have a dog," Roger's wife, Mary, sounded disappointed. "We were hoping you had a dog. The Chartrands, who had the house before you, had a big dog." Our over-the-fence conversation had turned from a general introduction to the neighbourhood to a gossip-fest about the local rowdies and now to Fortress Knox—our version of the better-known Fort.

"No," I replied. "But we do have cats."

"What do cats do against thieves?"

I had no answer to that.

"We were hoping you'd have a big scary dog. We've never gotten robbed when the Chartrands were here because Cub always barked at strangers. We're too old to have a dog. It's too much work for us, and for the Winters across the road too. So there's no dog in the neighbourhood now. We'll have to be really careful."

I wasn't sure how to read this. Was Mary expecting *us* to get a dog to protect *them?* Tony and I are both cat people. Getting a dog would almost be anathema.

"Yes," I felt it best to agree. I didn't want to tell her that we'd fallen in to the habit of leaving the front door wide open when we went out. "We'll all keep our eyes open." For what, I wasn't sure.

"Good," she replied. "We all keep an eye on each others' homes around here. An unofficial neighbourhood watch. It's safest that way." This pastoral neighbourhood was beginning to sound like South Central L.A.

"Surely, people don't wear guns here?" The closest thing we had was a bicycle pump. A poor equalizer, if ever there was.

"Oh no!" She was shocked at the thought. "But nearly everybody has a shotgun for hunting."

I made a mental note not to make any unplanned visits after dark, just in case, and we began a sporadic watch on our neighbours. Our open-door habit proved to be harder to break than we thought. If it wasn't wide open, it was unlocked. If the front door was locked, the back door was open. And let's not even mention the windows…

One morning, Tony and I woke to find the Ontario Provincial Police in Roger's driveway.

"How unusual," I said to Tony. "I didn't think they patrolled around here very often."

"They don't," he replied, nose glued to the kitchen window. "Something's going on. Roger's out there too and he doesn't look very happy. I'll go and be neighbourly."

"My garage got broken into," Roger roared at Tony in his customary tone. He was hopping mad, literally, and red like a tomato. Tony stepped back a few feet for the benefit of his eardrums and hoped that Roger was either taking blood pressure medication or that his plaid shirt was reflecting onto his face. "Look! Someone cut around the lock with a saw so now there's this huge great hole in the door. They took all my power tools and a freezerful of meat. I didn't hear a gosh-darn thing from the bedroom. Fine way to start the day—a call to the insurance company. This would never have happened if there was a dog around here..."

Or a burglar alarm linked to a response service.

hell hath no fury like a septic tank ignored

Y'know," the Chartrands told us when they handed over the keys to the house. "You might consider having the septic tank drained fairly soon."

"Really?" we asked. "Why so pressing?"

"Well, we're here ten years and we never had it done. There's so much information out there about how often to do it, we just didn't bother. It works fine. Besides, you'll need to dig up the trap door."

There was no sign of any trap in the yard. We pointed this out.

"We'll leave you the map," they assured us.

Judging by the lush grass in the leach field in the middle of a dry summer, we concurred that sooner would be better than later. Out came the map, shovels and tape measure one sunny morning.

"We should be done in about an hour," predicted Tony, leaning his lanky frame nonchalantly on a shovel. "Then I'm going fishing."

It was not to be. With the benefit of hindsight, I bet the Chartrands searched high and low for the trap and just gave up. The information on the map looked fine at first glance, but a closer look revealed some inaccuracies.

So we, too, searched high and low for the tank. First, we had to decipher the numbers. Eights looked exactly like threes; fives bore an uncanny resemblance to sixes. We measured in feet and inches, and when that failed, in metres; then by carefully examining the right angles and applying Pythagoras's theorem; then we thought that it would be better to go by the landscaping features shown—then we threw away the map! Mounds of earth had sprouted like mushrooms around the yard where we had tried and failed, digging down into impenetrable clay and hardpan to no avail.

While Tony leaned a little less nonchalantly on his shovel, I went to see Roger, next door.

"Oh yes," he shouted at the top of his voice. Roger must think everybody in the world is stone deaf. I have yet to hear him speak in anything close to normal volume, never mind *pianissimo*. "I remember when it was done. The backhoe got stuck in the mud and had to be hauled out by a tractor."

The incident must have amused him no end. He gave a couple of great belly laughs that made his great belly heave up and down in rhythm with the guffaws. So that explained the deep trenches remaining in the lawn to this day but was no help for our current predicament.

"Okay, Roger," I said in an attempt to refocus the conversation. "Do you remember who the plumber was?"

"Yes," came the reply. "But he's been dead these fifteen years."

I felt my jaw tighten. The plumber's demise was probably just as well. I would have had some spicy words for him on account of that map. No sober man could possibly have written down such utter fiction in the guise of useful data.

"Do you remember who owned the house when the work was done?" I asked.

"Vanderveen."

The very same fellow who had severed the farm and made a fistful of cash in the process. At last, we were getting somewhere. Roger even had a current phone number for him.

"Well," said Vanderveen. "I don't remember exactly where but I know it's behind the house."

I sighed.

"Jasper Buchanan's daughter was there watching. You could try her," he suggested. Jasper bought his place, three doors up from ours, in the twenties. Local folklore says he's the only person on this section of road to have paid his farm off by actually farming. His daughter moved away years ago. I wondered why on earth Vanderveen thought she would remember if he himself couldn't.

John Hennessy, two doors up, lent us a steel rod that we were to pound into the ground here and there in the faint hope of hitting the hollow sound of the tank lid. We dug down six or seven times, again to no avail. The yard was taking on the appearance of a minefield. It was a disgrace.

Sal Russo, one of my McGill colleagues, suggested we use SONAR. While the idea had its technical merits, we didn't think the local hardware store would have one for rent. I berated him gently for thinking too much like an engineer. Finally, only one course of action was left open to us—to follow the pipe from the house and add a huge scar to the mushrooms.

It took us all summer but we did find the tank, cleverly hidden in the warm embrace (or choking stranglehold, according to your outlook on life) of the roots of a huge Manitoba maple.

When the sewage truck operator lifted the trap, we were greeted by a heaving mass of pink frothy stuff—millimetres from the top. Fascinating. We had narrowly avoided an explosion that would have shredded the neighbourhood!

Summer turned to autumn and the mists rolled in gently from the St. Lawrence River every evening. The view from the living room window took on an uncanny resemblance to *The Hound of the Baskervilles*—the gaping, grave-sized hole under a tree, the loose earth piled on one side with a shovel sticking out of it, and the whole scene capped by the distant howling of coyotes.

There was no need to dress up for Halloween that year. We had the makings of a horror movie in our very own back yard. Had there been more kids in the neighbourhood, we would have charged an entrance fee.

front-page news: a criminal investigation

There is a serial killer in our midst.

the clues

One: a disturbing collection of chicken-coloured feathers outside the run one morning. Somebody, probably she-who-always-goes-to-bed-late, wasn't in when Tony locked the coop door. She perched unprotected near the door as far into the night as she got.

Two: some very distinctive paw prints at the bottom of the water trough. Do we need the crime scene unit to record the evidence? Deduction: the "perp" can leap or climb a high chicken-wire fence and has long toes and claws.

Three: on recent mornings, one fewer duck or chicken has emerged from Matt's collection of critters at the horse barn across the road from our house. Their mandate is to clean up any spilled grain and avoid giving rodents a free meal, so they're not locked up at night like our girls are.

Four: sometimes the "perp" enjoys his victim elsewhere and there is neither an obvious crime scene or a victim to autopsy, unlike the widely scattered duck carcass from the last evisceration. One might counter that an autopsy might prove inconclusive due to the many missing parts. Deduction: whoever the "perp" is, he's a butcher, not a surgeon.

Five: Matt informed us that his cat- and dog-food supply had been consumed—but not by his cats and dog.

We have a suspect based on circumstantial evidence and witnesses are helping us with our investigation.

a scream in the night

Exactly that. We were rudely woken by a desperate scream—the kind you think you've heard but aren't quite sure if you were dreaming, and by the time your brain wakes up, you'll never know. We were freaked enough to rush out in our undies to investigate.

The beam from the flashlight revealed the crumpled body of Matt's Rhode Island Red rooster in front of the barn door—a brightly coloured little thing whose diminutive size and lack of standing in the pecking order didn't stop it from trying to get to first base with our girls.

caught red-handed

A rustle in the nearby tree. The "perp" is still at the crime scene! Tony shone the flashlight up, catching the reflection from a pair of masked eyes, very reminiscent of cartoon burglars. A monster raccoon.

Front page headlines on next day's early edition: ASSASSIN IDENTIFIED, MAKES GETAWAY THROUGH TREES. AUTHORITIES UNABLE TO KEEP UP.

victim mauled... but survives

The heap of feathers lay silent, but breathing. Tony gave it a vague prod with his foot to check for life-affirming reactions. The rooster exploded into action with a velocity and blood-curdling scream that knocked us back in astonishment. If ever a meal was crying to be eaten, this was it. Utterly panicked and screaming like a banshee, the poor creature scooted around like that proverbial chicken. The lights in Roger's bedroom window flicked on. This would not be a banner night for neighbourhood relations. A veteran country-dweller, Roger must have known from some unfathomable idiomatic wisdom that this was the most mosquito-infested night of the year to date. That, or seeing that we were already on site of something he didn't want to be involved in, he decided to do what normal humans do in the middle of the night. The lights switched off again and Roger returned to the kind of deep slumber we wouldn't be experiencing that night. Instead, Tony and I carved our way through Matt's sopping wet hay fields in our slippers and undies, chasing a screeching rooster who, for an injured person, was doing a magnificent job of evading capture.

residents advised to lock their doors

If I thought I was being deafened before, the rooster cranked up the volume several more notches once I actually got my hands on him. How can there be such capacity in such small lungs?

We brought the victim into the porch, which was temporarily serving as a greenhouse, to recuperate. A good dose of quick-acting sedative would have been just the ticket as he ran amok through our seedlings. Is it possible to sue victims for financial compensation? In despair of getting any kind of sleep that night, Tony stuffed him into an open-ended sack with some grain and left him in the secure part of the run. Of course, the victim might now counter-sue for assault and kidnap.

Attempts to rescue any other animals from the barn who might serve as potential meals were stymied by the padlocked door.

victim recovering in hospital

The rooster suffered multiple injuries and severe trauma. His eyes were either glued together in fear or he was blinded by the killer. I wasn't sure that heaps of TLC in the intensive care unit the following morning would suffice. Would we need the ophthalmologist and/or the psychiatrist? Life in the country doesn't bode well for a blind rooster. Towards the end of the day, however, he had recovered enough to open both eyes and demand better room service.

perpetrator under siege

Matt promised to collect the victim and keep other residents safe by locking them in secure quarters at night. He also promised to borrow a live-trap. There is no more death penalty in Canada. This should be a straightforward case of exile to another part of the country.

the cat who came in from the cold

Cooney, and his unprepossessing name, wandered up the road from the McGillivray farm to live with us where there are more ample opportunities for professional development in the form of mice in the coop and better living conditions generally. He's a handsome, strapping Himalayan look-alike, far better suited to his neighbourhood nickname—*Brutus!*—the result of his scalloped-eared look and combative reputation.

When it became clear that our casa really was his casa, it became equally clear that he must be neutered.

"We have to plan this carefully so he does minimum travelling," I said. "Why don't we take him in for shots when our cats are due, then back two weeks later for the neutering?"

"And we'll lock him in the porch overnight to make sure he's there when we're ready to leave," replied Tony. "That won't be easy."

"I'll lock the cat-door on in-only and bait the porch with food. That should do the trick."

The morning of the appointment, the cat-door lay in a dozen scattered pieces on the porch. Cooney, snoozing peacefully on the outside step, opened one eye at me.

"Look what I did, Ma!" he smiled proudly. "It didn't work so I fixed it."

Cat-carriers have bad karma. We anticipated World War III to "wrassle" him into one, bearing in mind that we have to don gauntlets and protective goggles when handling our own cats. Their strength and weight increase in proportion with our frustration. They stiffen—akin to *rigor mortis*—into the shape of a star-jump edged with razor blades while our tendons strain under our skin like cheese wire to avoid the mortal swipes. Cooney was the easiest of the lot. A dollop of canned food in the back of the carrier and he walked right in.

The clinic was a twenty-minute drive away. With four cats on perpetual vomit-alert and wailing like a poorly rehearsed choir in the back, we voiced quiet regrets about the earplugs left on the kitchen counter.

"Can you smell that?" asked Tony.

"You know I don't have a good sense of smell, Hun," I replied. I sniffed the air to prove my point. "Well, actually… Yes, I can." Adding to the assault on our senses, a terrible odour slowly wafted toward the front seats. Tony gripped the steering wheel until the whites of his knuckles showed and stepped hard on the gas.

The receptionist at the clinic recoiled at the smell surrounding our party.

"Oh my goodness," she said sweetly. "That can't have been a pleasant trip."

The cats had metaphorical clothes pegs on their noses and pointed accusingly at Cooney.

"He did it. He did it."

Indeed, he did. And judging by the potency of the odour, multiple times. Tony took them all into the consulting room while I registered with the receptionist. He emerged, nostrils flared.

"You'd better get in here," he said flatly. "It's bad."

Through the door, I could see Cooney being held by the armpits at arm's length. He was sodden from stem to stern and dripping unspeakable liquids in various shades of brown. The vet was a brick. He helped us clean off this poor cat, the carrier, the floor, the examining table and every other surface Cooney had slithered onto as he tried to escape the smell that stuck to him like a shadow. I imagine that once we were gone, he conducted a massive disinfection campaign in the entire clinic and made an appropriate note in Cooney's file: nervous bowel.

"Poor Coon," I said, on the way back. "He trusted us and look what happened."

"Don't forget we're doing this again in two weeks' time. He can trust us then," said Tony. "Besides, I'll have to do something about the car. I can't drive around with that smell following me everywhere."

The trip for the neutering proved nowhere near as eventful, although the receptionist greeted our arrival with caution. Cooney grinned widely at her and behaved like a perfect gentleman.

The Coon was wasted as a barn cat. He's smart, funny and affectionate. He sits on our feet, purring like a well-maintained truck, sleeps on his back next to the wood stove snoring loudly and, tail high, leads the way to the coop, turning occasionally to make sure we're still behind him.

Of course we are. It's his casa.

where there's smoke, there's fire

As a throwback to the days before garbage collection, country-dwellers retain a fondness for burning whatever trash they can instead of sending it to the landfill. There are notable exceptions, such as dead tires, which it is most definitely *verboten* to burn. Instead, the Township asks for a financial contribution per tire for the privilege of allowing the landfill to "store" them safely.

"What on earth is Roger burning?" I wondered to nobody in particular. He had been smoking us out for three whole days.

"Oh, you mean that bitter smell?" replied Tony. "I think it's his old kitchen lino. I'm just glad we're up-wind."

"Jeez! I hope we don't have to smell it too much longer."

"Well, it won't be the last time unusual and inappropriate stuff gets burned around here, I'm sure. Everybody does it."

A reputation is easy to make, so needless to say, we blamed Roger for the musty, yet gamey, smell that percolated through the house one winter's day. It was a strange evening; inexplicable fog patches hung low and long even though it had snowed that day. Everything had a mystical translucent whiteness to it.

I trekked out to the coop to put the chickens to bed, trying hard to hold my breath on the way. Weird, I thought, to have such a large fog patch around the barn, even though it's in a low spot on the land. Strange, I mused as I approached, that here the fog is rolling upwards.

The compost heap caught the corner of my eye. The snow cover had melted to reveal a Kilimanjaro-like structure complete with sputtering crater with vents on the slopes releasing noxious fumes.

OMIGOD! THE COMPOST HEAP IS ON FIRE!

An expedition to the crater revealed that Tony had dumped the ashes from the wood stove onto the compost—which is fine—but had neglected to check that the all coals were out. The natural warmth of the decomposing pile, coupled with a topping of several months' worth of chicken droppings and straw, had created ideal conditions for combustion. I couldn't put it out with water—the line to the barn had frozen months ago. I flung myself onto the pile and stomped it out as best I could, kicking to make certain no embers were lurking in the ashes. This dance only served to fan the billowing smoke. I disappeared into a cloud of chicken-shit fumes. It just about choked me.

Back on the porch, Tony eyed me up and down.

"*What* have you been up to?" he asked.

"Don't ask," I replied dryly. My coat was still smoking. The smell wafting around me caught in his throat. I took off my melted rubber boots and headed inside. Tony blocked my way.

"Oh no," he said, waving one finger at me. "You're not coming in smelling like that, my friend. Strip!"

"You have got to be kidding."

He crossed his arms, standing rock-like in front of the door. I couldn't get by him. I grudgingly did a record-breaking striptease in the unheated porch, flinging my clothes outside as I went, and pushed past him into more bearable conditions for the scantily clad.

Roger's house was directly downwind that night. I wonder what he thought *we* were burning...

by the light of the wintry moon

The phone jolted us out of our reverie. It was ten o'clock on Christmas Eve.

"Is Tony there?" boomed a lusty set of pipes at the other end of the line. I jerked the receiver away from my ear. Big smile on his face and two rooms away, Tony could hear the conversation clearly.

"Just a moment."

"Never mind," bellowed the voice. "I can tell you instead."

"Charmed, I'm sure," I thought.

"There's a few horses loose in the road and one of them's fallen on the ice. You people, you know the feller better than us."

I was fairly certain it was Roger—mainly because of the volume—but since he hadn't introduced himself, I wasn't about to make a social *faux pas*.

"Who *is* this?" I managed to interject, as he paused for breath.

"It's Roger, next door," came the offended reply.

I wondered why he had even bothered with the telephone. The low-tech solution would have been to open the window and shout in our general direction. He proceeded to repeat the same information at the same volume. We were going in circles.

"I'll call Matt," I assured him. "Merry Christmas."

I peered through the porch window into the night. Two pairs of eyes looked right back at me and two pairs of nostrils snorted foggily.

"Tony, Tony," I cried. "Matt's horses have broken out from across the road. One of them has fallen on the road already and who knows where the others are. They could be hit by any one of the maniacs who treat this road like a race track."

Tony jumped into his boots and coat while I called Matt.

"Hello," he replied cheerfully to my greeting. He was wrapping Christmas gifts. His face must have blanched when I told him because, after a brief silence, his next phrase was so very soft.

"Thanks for calling. I'll be right there." Click.

Matt lives in Ingleside. "Right there" is a good fifteen-minute drive away.

In the meantime, Tony and I presented the two horses with a smorgasbord of apples, carrots, lettuce and broccoli. Any equine with a discerning palate should have been delighted. For vegetarians accustomed to a limited menu of hay and grass, however, they were singularly uninterested. All they wanted to do was lean against us.

"Mind your toes," said Tony, wryly observing the little rubber boots that had already suffered a meltdown on the compost pile. "I bet horses don't look too closely at what they're stepping on. I'm not spending Christmas Eve in a hospital waiting room."

So far, he'd spent the evening watching *It's a Wonderful Life* for the thousandth time. The difference would be marginal.

Something spooked the horse resting its chin on my head and it galloped off into the ice-blue field faster than we could follow through the snowdrifts.

"You know," I told Tony, somewhat spooked myself at seeing teeth and hooves at such close range. "This could have been so much easier had they been wearing halters."

As I beat my way through the snow in a lukewarm pursuit, I noticed what a glorious night it was. I paused to catch my breath and savour the poetry of the moment. Here we were, Christmas Eve, under this incredible sky filled with myriad stars and a blazing full moon. And in the middle distance, a white horse disappearing into the blanched landscape.

The sound of a truck careening down the road brought me back to reality. Matt had plucked his girlfriend's son out of bed, correctly guessing that an eleven year old in pyjamas with slippers inside his rubber boots would be more useful than the two of us. They returned the escapees to the paddock where they discovered that the gate had failed. With freedom within their grasp, all the horses had done was cross the road. Home must be where the hay is.

"Holy Shmoly," said Matt, quite puffed from the exertion, blond locks sticking out from his toque at right angles. "It'd almost be worth building a house on this land right next to the barn just so we could keep a better eye on these guys. I can't be driving back and forth like this from home in Ingleside. It's nuts!"

We agreed and chatted a while longer in the crisp air, debating the best location for his dream home before returning to the endless *It's a Wonderful Life*.

Betcha nobody does this on Christmas Eve in downtown Montreal.

the novelty-of-farmin'-wears-off years

noah's ark

The sight that awaited Tony when he opened the coop door on that first warm spring morning was one of disaster and devastation.

"Jeez!" he exclaimed. He closed the door, blinked, and slowly opened it again.

Nothing had changed. The chickens were still up to their bellies in freezing cold water. The feeder was still submerged. The drinking pail was long gone. The aquarium heater to keep their drinking water warm still floated in somebody's wake. Empty nesting boxes were still bobbing up and down like unanchored boats. Some of the girls, confused into inaction, clung to the relative safety of those nesting boxes still hanging on the wall. Overnight, shin-deep meltwater had turned the coop into a pond. And there's no such thing as a chicken pond—or a duck coop.

This was not the way we had envisioned keeping chickens. We wanted happy, healthy birds. Birds who didn't get picked up by their necks or feet, and didn't get made into soup at the end of their egg-producing days. Birds who enjoyed the great outdoors. Not poor, soggy creatures with colds and rheumatism.

Back at the house, Tony ripped his keys off the side table and ran to the car.

"The chickens have stopped asking for blankets and thermal underwear," he said on his way, in reference to the fact that the coop is unheated. "They've put in a written request, in triplicate, for a hammer, nails and boards to build an Ark. I'm off to buy a sump pump. It's urgent!"

"An Ark? A sump pump? What happened?" I asked. Too late. Tony was halfway to Ingleside.

In Year One of the Chickens, the girls arrived in May. In preparation for their arrival, we refurbished one of the rooms in the barn, insulated it with straw, levelled the floor (and in the process uncovered what I thought for sure was a coffin, but turned out to be a sheet of plywood!) and cleaned out a secure, fenced run. Our new coop looked good. Little did we know.

"That barn was twice the size back then," Roger, next door, informed us later on in the season, when we asked for a bit of history. It had been his parents' farm in the Thirties. "They only used it for storing equipment because it's so low. It's totally useless for anything else." His voice filled the cathedral ceiling in the kitchen like a cathedral organ. I wasn't about to disclose that we were using it for animals.

As the day warmed—perfect for melting away winter—the pump ran non-stop. Tony and I bailed like drowning sailors. The water level rose... and rose...

"It's all right for you," said Tony during a short break. "You're going back to town. I'm going to be stuck here bailing freezing cold, smelly, brown liquid for the next several weeks."

I chose not to mention the same, smelly, brown streak up his face or the muck plastering his coat.

"We'll just do what we can," I replied. A wave of that stuff licked the top of my boots and seeped down to my toes. I wasn't having any fun either.

Relief came in the form of a cold snap. I never thought I'd hear myself say that. The water turned to mush then to ice. The girls learned to skate, arriving en masse at the feeder like a demolition derby. Throughout this difficult period, they laid the usual number of eggs. We heaped praise on them and increased their rations.

The weather warmed again; the fields melted; the girls did chicken-paddle. Tony and the pump each bailed some three hundred litres of water every day. He silently prayed for a way out. This time, relief came in the form of Susie, his practical sister.

"Why have you been bailing all this time?" she asked, not believing her ears. "You have the materials out there. Build bridges for them."

An idea so simple, so brilliant, we kicked ourselves for not thinking of it before. So we did just that—planks on piles of bricks leading to and from key areas. Effective it was. Aesthetic it certainly was not. The girls relaxed, dried off and put away their life jackets. Their own efforts at boat building had come to naught.

As the days grew longer and the sun warmed their backs, the girls revelled in being outside. New grass poked its way through the snow, the crocuses were in flower and the blackbirds and Canada geese were already back from their winter quarters.

Now I know the true meaning of "spring thaw."

an object in motion tends to stay in motion

So said Einstein. Obviously, he never drove any of our cars.

"That car isn't worth scrap metal any more," said Tony about our dear little 1989 Mazda 323. He washed the grease from his hands purposefully. He'd done enough work on it to know. The metaphor was clear.

Personally, I thought it was a workhorse. It spent many years dealing with Montreal's infamous potholes, into which many vehicles vanish never to emerge. It shouldered the move to the country, carried hundreds of kilos of chicken feed as well as several hundred patio bricks given to us by Joan Alexander after she renovated her deck. Tony insisted these bricks cooked the shocks and the car was never the same again.

When we replaced it with the Volkswagen Jetta, we were looking forward to a trouble-free ride. The Jetta had been ostensibly well looked after and had many features that would bring us almost up to date with automotive technology.

"I'll shave a few dollars off the sale price," said the owner, at which point we should have smelled the citrus. "I haven't had time to get the wheels balanced."

"You can't balance wheels with damaged rims," the mechanic at the local garage told us. "And these are aluminum rims. Really good quality. The only place that will repair them is in Quebec City."

As we shelled out three hundred dollars for this first of many repairs and drove the car on winter tires in the middle of a September heat wave, we wondered what else the former owner might have neglected to mention.

We soon found out that reliability was whimsical. The alternator failed; Tony drove back from Cornwall in the middle of a blizzard without windshield wipers or heat. Various belts failed; one causing him to walk home from Ingleside in his pyjamas—again in winter—after dropping off some mail. It was this particular incident that made him break the habit of only dressing after he'd done half a day's work. The clutch cable broke, bringing the car to a complete standstill. Coincidentally, our CAA membership expired the day before. Tony managed to engage reverse gear and backed all the way home from Ingleside, to the amazement of the few onlookers the countryside has to offer and the Canada geese honking overhead. He was fully dressed for that particular incident, otherwise the neighbours might have felt a tad nervous. Then the front seal on the power steering let go, doubtless in sympathy with the rest of the car.

On one Monday crack-of-dawn commute to Montreal, we got as far as the s-bend on Knox Road when the car started choking. As we slowly and cursingly pushed the car homewards past a cluster of houses, a retired gentleman emerged.

"I bet we can take care of this," he took charge of the situation and towed us into his driveway.

The hood went up and two heads disappeared into the engine.

"The distributor cap is wet," he said.

"It's toast, more like," replied Tony, staring at it with tangible annoyance.

"For now, we'll use a hairdryer and at least you can be on your way."

Tony had to be in Cornwall for eight-thirty after dropping me off at the train station in Dorion, Quebec. I'd missed all the commuter trains from Dorion into downtown Montreal that would save him driving me all the way. The next available VIA train got me to McGill at one o'clock. My colleagues didn't bat an eyelid. Universities are a haven for non-linear employees.

"You'll never guess what's wrong with the car now," he said over the phone to me at Joan's a few days later. "The battery has developed an electrical drain. I got caught out a couple of times and had to ask some kind strangers to lift their hood. I keep the tractor battery in the car now. It never ends!"

Indeed, it turned out that the starter was finished. A new one fixed the problem but a week later, the exhaust pipe fell off.

The icing on the cake came on another Monday morning commute to Montreal. A barely audible tick-tick turned into a thunderous knocking. Montreal drivers lived up to their reputation as a pitiless lot. They stared stonily at the hapless occupants who dared to slow down rush hour traffic on the expressway. Our collective blood pressure soared as cars passed us like we were standing still. Tony inched the car up the off-ramp where it slumped and died. The head had broken. Whatever that means in technical terms, in practical terms, it meant that we walked the remaining two kilometres to McGill with sixteen dozen eggs on our backs without making an omelette on the sidewalk in the process.

Two weeks and all our savings later, the Jetta was better but not perfectly healthy. This time, Tony was right. The car was never the same again. He swears our next vehicle will be brand spanking new and straight from the dealer's lot.

the sting

Tony showed me the dent in the riding mower caused by a head-on collision with a tree. Then he showed me the red welt between his shoulder blades and the connection between the two was instantly clear.

"They're just bugs being bugs, sweetie," I said.

"Well, they can be just bugs somewhere else," came his terse reply, as he manoeuvred into position to scratch that itch on the same poor tree.

Of course, had we done our homework properly when buying the house, we would have known that the area is made up of big, swampy wetlands that any self-respecting mosquito would call a very comfortable home. If, as advised, we had talked to the locals before placing our offer to purchase, Roger, next door, could have told us why our neighbourhood is filled with both water- and insect-loving birds. Come each spring, it's one of my great pleasures to see the meltwater in low-lying fields provide a temporary habitat for thousands of Canada geese and say, "Look. Geese swimming in a field." Small things amuse small minds... Later on in the season, it's another great pleasure to see those same hayfields, now lush and verdant, provide cover for (probably) the same geese who now look like umbrella-heads poking above the grasses.

"I'll get the calamine," I said, observing the pretty array of splotches already dabbed on the festering sores covering his arms and legs. We buy calamine by the barrel.

"It's time to come in anyway," he replied, squinting into the fading light.

The countdown to dusk had begun and our time in the garden was limited. It mattered not that the lawn was only half mowed. We threw down our tools and ran for cover. Once again, we would enjoy the flaming sunset from behind closed doors.

"It's such a shame," I mused. "We're forced to work outside under the beating midday sun and the gnats get to enjoy the beautiful evenings."

Tony's acknowledgement came in the form of a grunt. He had contorted his lean physique into a pretzel, the better to scratch the day's collection of bites. His mind was elsewhere.

Of course, we could be using DEET, efficient product that it is. But its reputation—equal to that of Agent Orange—doesn't fit our organic lifestyle choices. On the other hand, there were many little bottles of snakeskin oil available that promised to work wonders. Our first proud purchase was an itch-preventer that had to be applied within fifteen minutes of being stung.

"Ouch. I've been bitten. Where's the stuff?"

"It's in my pocket. Let me finish planting this seedling. Hmm, maybe it's not in my pocket... Oh yes, it's in my other dungarees."

"Where are they?"

"In the laundry."

"Too late. Forget it."

So we went the prevention route instead: citronella oil. We slithered easily into our work clothes and went bravely forward into the field. A miracle! Citronella really does work. But only for about half an hour, then we had to re-apply and just as liberally.

"What's wrong?"

I could barely look at Tony. The oil reflected the sun like a mirror. On a man blessed with so many freckles over a milky-white skin, I wondered if a primer coat of sunscreen would be well advised.

"My hands are too slippery. I can't hold on to the tools properly."

Nor could we hold on to a cool drink or work up a lather in the shower. Citronella has limited uses.

"I'm gonna outwit those little vampires if it's the last thing I do." His jaw set and his eyes hardened. These were not just clues. They were a telltale giveaway that Tony was in battle-mode.

"No more shorts and t-shirts for me!"

"What! Naked?"

"No! Sleeves and long pants."

"Phew. In this heat?" I was sceptical.

Topped by a mosquito net over our heads, we thought victory was in sight. I, for one, died a thousand deaths under all those clothes on the torrid days, and the headgear made us look like aliens. Tony, stubborn like a mule in his pseudo-victory, concentrated on the weeding while peals of laughter from passing cars rippled in our direction. Roger was more considerate. He actually asked us where he might buy one for himself. Personally, I think he went back inside and howled in the privacy of his own home.

Next year, we're trying a new system.

"These are going to save us," said Tony, opening up the contents of a mail-order envelope to reveal two expensive, battery-operated, wristwatch-type things. He just won't give up, will he?

"They emit the sound of the male mosquito's wings," he explained. "It's supposed to keep the females away. They're the ones that bite."

I'm not sure why it should work. But if it does, I swear I'll buy a controlling share in the company. It'll still be cheaper than all that calamine.

the soft touch

"Have you chicken?" one of our McGill sharers asked me. English was not his first language, or his second.

"Yes, forty-eight of them," I replied.

"I buy one," he continued, raising one finger in emphasis.

"You want to buy a chicken?" I questioned dubiously.

"Yes, one chicken," he confirmed.

"Buy… one… chicken…" I repeated slowly, still completely fogged. I was sure there were municipal bylaws against keeping farm animals in town.

"Yes!" He too was beginning to look puzzled. Was I selling or wasn't I?

"Don't you get it?" Peter Kuhns, overhearing this ships-in-the-night conversation on his way to the coffee pot, couldn't stand it any longer. "He wants *meat*."

Peter, one of the engineering profs, occupied an office across the hall from mine. A master of procrastination, the big man would wander into my neck of the woods for hot liquids, candy and general conversation on a regular basis. With an unparalleled memory for trivia as well as the know-how to fix my computer, I was always glad to see him. He was also one of Harvest Moon Farm's staunchest sharers.

My internal light switched on.

"Ohhhhh. You want *chicken*."

The sharer looked relieved.

I cast my mind a hundred and forty kilometres away to where the girls were having a dust bath in the compost or sunning themselves under the lean-to. It was a good life.

This dilemma had reared its ugly head before. Second-year layers generally end up in the pot—even if they are only good enough for soup or stew by then—simply because a superficial cost analysis of keeping them ends in a flow of red ink.

I had spoken to Dan Flansbury, our organically-inclined crony, about having somebody come in to "do the deed."

"Do it yourself," he suggested. "Otherwise the price of the meat won't cover the cost of the Guillotine Man."

Neither Tony nor I was prepared to "do it ourselves." That was the whole point. Dan refused to accept how squeamish I was about terminating animal lives. He raises chickens, turkeys, cows, pigs and bison for slaughter on his farm, not for pets. We would never see eye to eye on this.

My mind worked overtime on finding a solution. I started calling petting zoos—not top of my list for alternative lifestyles for the girls.

"Bring them in," said the owner of one.

"How long will you keep them?" I asked, relieved at solving the problem.

"Until they stop laying," he replied.

I sighed and hung up the phone.

To hell with economics! I hadn't turned to vegetarianism just so I could kill chickens for other people to eat. That winter, the girls ballooned under a thick coat of glossy feathers.

Temperatures down to minus fifteen degrees or thereabouts in the coop didn't faze them at all. They drank "hot toddies" thanks to the aquarium heater in their water and laid enough eggs to keep themselves in mash, and us in pocket money.

Come spring, we again felt unable to end their days—our justification being that they were even older and tougher. The eggs were gargantuan now and the sharers oohed and aaahed with pleasure. The girls were here to stay.

The arrival of a crop of young chickens put a definite kink in the pecking order—a kink that the old birds battled hard to redress. Somehow, Missy ended up on the bottom rung of the ladder. She was limping, severely wounded at the wing and the others terrorized her whenever she approached the feeder. We penned and fed her separately. She flourished under the individual attention although the limp never quite healed.

With the approach of colder nights the following autumn and the need to huddle for warmth, the time came for Missy to reintegrate with the flock. As she stood between our legs for protection, the girls clucked around us to identify the newcomer. Chickens aren't known for their long-term memory. Missy froze in fear. A scoop of mash scattered on the ground solved the crowding problem and she felt brave—or hungry—enough to join in. Nobody even looked at her. Missy was one of the gang again. And here was somebody who wanted to eat her!

Back in the hallowed halls of higher education, Peter's voice woke me from my reverie.

"I wouldn't bother asking these guys for meat," he advised the sharer, all the while contemplating his coffee mug. "Those chickens get wheelchairs for their golden years."

feed 'n weed... or feed the weeds

I used to tend my tiny community garden in Montreal meticulously. It rewarded those hours of care by blossoming into a perfect, prissy little plot. There was no way a single weedy trespasser was going to suck the lifeblood out of my precious vegetables. I brought that approach with me to our wide-open fields, tickled constantly, as they were, by the west wind laden with dandelion and other seeds. It didn't—it *couldn't*—last long.

"I wonder why the Chartrands never ran the mower into the northwest corner of the yard," I wondered aloud.

"Because riding mowers don't do right angles," replied Tony.

"Yeah, but…" I wasn't satisfied with that answer and I certainly wasn't satisfied with the tangled knot of spaghetti-like vines, brambles and hairy weeds growing gangbusters in that corner. I attributed the vigorous growth to the proximity of the leach field and its nutritious runoff.

"That'll be my next project." I've always liked right angles.

The largest tool at my command in Montreal had been a hand trowel. The crowbar—destined to become my favourite gardening tool at Harvest Moon Farm—promoted me into an entirely different category. With my straw hat tilted at a jaunty angle, my construction gloves, my filthy dungarees and this heavy steel bar in my hands, I felt invincible.

"I am woman. I am strong." I raised my puny arms in anticipated victory. I could barely sustain the weight of the crowbar. This was a mighty tool. Finally, I understood the power of machismo.

I hacked at those vines and roots with the aggression worthy of a mobster. The vegetation put up a good, but dirty, fight. It had time to regenerate between blows. It was two years before I raised my arms in victory again. The crowbar felt as light as a feather.

We also had to wrest control of our neglected fields from encroaching willows and other invasive flora. The southeast field was full of nothing useful, yet it was the perfect one to use for vegetables. I begged Dan to plough it for us.

"No problem," he said. "You use the part you want, and I'll seed the rest with buckwheat to choke out the weeds. Then it'll be fine for next year."

Well, Dan seeded nothing. As a result, we unintentionally grew an acre and a half of ragweed right beside our vegetable beds. If there were a market for ragweed—especially organic ragweed—we'd be millionaires. Conflicting emotions brewed inside me: a deep shame at our agricultural inadequacies; an equal relief that we didn't have enough neighbours to make a fuss about allergens and expensive fines; and that familiar desire to leap at Dan's throat to wipe off the grin. It certainly wasn't our fault that each time he promised faithfully to do the work, there was a mechanical issue to deal with. Dan has the same kind of luck with his tractor as we do with cars. In all fairness, the tractor did spend the better part of a week in our northwest field after some essential steel rod bent like a hairpin. No amount of punishment with a mallet could straighten it out. I made a mental note never to entrust repairs that required a modicum of finesse to him.

Anyway, the birds loved this unexpected food source. The cats loved that the birds loved it and grew fat on the proceeds. The following year, Dan seeded a handsome crop of golden oats. My shame, the quantity of bird carcasses on the lawn and the cats' waistlines all shrank.

All lessons in the vegetable garden were learned the hard way. During a drought, nothing grew—plants or weeds, but come a wet spring, the weeds definitely had the upper hand.

A quick glance at my bed of early carrots revealed a green fuzz of seedlings.

"Looks good, dear," said Tony. "That'll be a great bunch of Bugs Bunny carrots."

I didn't have the heart to tell him that I had no clue which were carrots and which were not. Greenhorn that I was, I had scattered the seeds over the bed instead of planting in rows.

"Oh," he said, pausing to pluck something that resembled a rubber plant. "You have some weeds in here."

"Yes. We'll have to spend a bit of time looking after those." The cruelty of that response quashed my irritation that he might have found me out.

I hoped that by procrastinating another week, the difference between young ragweed and young carrots might be more apparent. It was, but not in a good way. I showed Tony an example of the two.

"What's the difference?" he asked.

"Not much really. This bigger stuff needs to come out. The spindly stuff stays in. Otherwise, it looks the same."

A week of ensuing rain curbed any desire to venture back into the mud. By that time, the ragweed was waist high and in full bloom. The carrots, beets and radishes were but a distant memory—a few rotting stems under a lush canopy of seedy weeds. The season was a washout—literally.

The "rubber plant" Tony yanked from among the carrots was milkweed. I gasped involuntarily.

"You know the monarch butterflies you like so much?" I asked him later. "Well, milkweed is the only thing they eat. Because it's poisonous, consuming it makes *them* poisonous to predators."

"Oh," replied Tony. "We'd better leave it then, right?"

"It would be nice for them to have organic poison, wouldn't it, before they go down to Mexico?"

Who knows where my logic was that day but it was a decision I came to regret. Milkweed propagates aggressively and is almost impossible to eradicate once it has em"bedded" itself. On seeing how abundantly it grows in the local ditches along with the more beautiful orange day lilies, yellow goldenrod and bright blue chicory, I made a unilateral decision—there's plenty enough to go around without any living in *my* vegetables too. It got a head start on me, but I'm slowly winning that war.

No wonder the faint-of-heart look rather longingly at those herbicides.

bunny in dog's clothing

In Britain, sheepdog trials are the stuff of prime time TV. Like darts or snooker, only even more soporific. Brits understand the value of a highly trained sheepdog and look after them preciously.

Not to be outdone in the wilds of Ingleside, we too can claim a talented animal, ready for fame, fortune and the celluloid spotlight.

Among the members of Matt's unofficial petting zoo are two plain white Pekin ducks, a beautiful iridescent black duck (these being the remains of the raccoon-decimated flock), a white Barbary cob with a nasty look in his eye who doesn't hang out with the others and one white bunny with a brown-from-digging-in-the-dirt nose.

In harmony with Matt's flowing blond locks, *laissez-faire* personality and apparent come-and-go lifestyle, his chickens, ducks, bunnies and cats have a similar come-and-go lifestyle between their gypsy-like barn and our place. To our chagrin, they all hang out at the "local"—our birdfeeder—waiting, mouth agape, to catch whatever the chickadees and sparrows splash out. The ducks, habitually rising at the crack of dawn, run across the road first. The bunny probably sleeps in a little because by the time he arrives, the best vantage points are taken and it's tough to get a seed in edgeways. It would be a lot easier if those big birds weren't around…

So Mr. Bunny herds the early-birds round… and round… until they're so dizzy they don't care where they are. They quack at him, sit on him and peck furiously on his head; round… and round…; he winds left, feigns right, deeks left again; round… and round…; pushes them occasionally with his head; round… and round…

By the time their brains have stopped spinning, they've been zigzagged back across the road and into their own yard. Meanwhile, under our feeder sits Mr. Bunny, smiling and waiting for his reward to fall upon him.

"We should send this in to Letterman," cried Tony in amusement. "You know, the Stupid Pet Tricks segment he puts on sometimes. I bet he doesn't get many bunnies this clever."

Matt probably doesn't know that Brits would pay real money to have Mr. Bunny on their sheep farm. Letterman's lack of appreciation was a disappointment. We never heard back.

stop, thief!

Tony and I picked up some basic principles of country life very quickly. Others we had to learn the hard way. Feeding the wildlife comes under the latter heading.

The northeast field is my favourite, in spite of the junk pile left behind by generations of owners at which we are slowly whittling away. It boasts a short path leading into the bush as far as a human can go without needing a machete. Prickly ash flourishes in that particular spot. On an early foray, we found ourselves gripped in the thorns like criminals in barbed wire and emerged in tatters. Apparently, the bark is an excellent analgesic but I find it more convenient to pop an aspirin. Tucked away behind the other fields, the deer love the seclusion and the russet apple tree growing in a small thicket in the middle. It's too far to walk for a small, maggoty apple so we donated the tree to them.

The deer visit the pond in the southwest field as well, but in the absence of other tracks, we assumed they kept to their well-worn paths. We even gloated over our neighbours who bemoaned their deer issues to us. We were footloose and deer-free. Our deer were exemplary. Come autumn…

"If I didn't know better," said Tony, gazing into our apple tree one fine afternoon. "I'd swear there are fewer apples today than yesterday."

"Well," I countered, bent over some very clear hoof prints. "I'd say you don't know better and that we have a problem."

"We certainly do," he replied, although the problem he was focusing on—the apples—was somewhat narrower than mine—the entire vegetable garden. "It's going to take two ladders roped together and a stick to prod down what's left."

Whatever precarious scaffolding of ladders, glue, duct tape and safety pins he wanted to assemble to reach a few apples, I didn't want to know. Sooner or later, they would fall of their own accord and I would make apple sauce. Simple. I crossed to the other side of the house to check on the garden. It looked different somehow...

Tony heard the yell of laughter and came running. I pointed to the bed of broccoli.

"I couldn't figure it out from a distance," I choked between giggles. "I thought the plants looked rather thin."

Every last leaf had been carefully plucked, leaving the stalks standing bolt upright—utterly naked! The broccoli harvest was mostly done so I wasn't that bothered. I was, however, much perturbed by the carrot bed that had been razed to the ground.

"Do you know how much work it's going to be to harvest those carrots?" I lectured Tony, who really didn't deserve it. "Have you tried pulling topless carrots? Do you know how hard it is?"

"About as hard as harvesting topless beets, I'd say," he replied from the beet bed.

I went "beet" red with frustration.

"Y'don't say! We need a really good deterrent next year. Let's think on it over the winter."

This was beginning to sound like a *déjà-vu* of our mosquito experience. I lost faith.

❧ ❧ ❧ ❧ ❧ ❧ ❧ ❧

"Why do these tomatoes always have holes?" I wondered aloud, after picking a bountiful harvest.

"I know," agreed Tony. "And they're all from the same bed. Maybe there's a deficiency in the soil or something."

I wasn't prepared to argue about soil deficiencies being so localized as to affect one bed of tomatoes but not another, so I let the matter drop. Unsellable, they became a very excellent salsa for our own consumption instead. Time came to uproot the plants and mulch the beds for winter. From the corner of my eye, I saw Squirtie-cat, who was helping that day, pounce lightning-fast into the straw and surface with a mouse. A tomato-loving mouse. A tomato-loving mouse in great danger of contributing to Squirtie's expanding girth. A tomato-loving mouse who needed rescuing and who was about to be relocated deep, deep into the woods.

❧ ❧ ❧ ❧ ❧ ❧ ❧ ❧

It never occurred to Tony that feeding the raccoons would have consequences. After all, our friend Joan, in Montreal, fed her masked visitors a gourmet *mélange* of cat food and eggs on the porch, after which they would curl up in the cat beds to digest and even excuse themselves politely after burping.

"Look," whispered Tony one evening, pointing at several pairs of eyes reflecting the living room light. "I think it's a mother and her kits."

It was indeed. She was demonstrating to her young family how to climb the tree to the bird feeder and scatter the seed like a fountain. Tony was charmed. So started a nightly routine of a saucepan full of birdseed, milk and bread that the youngsters would overturn and scarf down with loud munching noises and the odd snort. No table manners in the country, I tell you.

"Look," he called me over again, visibly melting at one of the kits begging on its hind legs at the back door. "Isn't he so cute!"

"You wanna be careful with them," advised John Hennessy. "The girls fed some a few years ago and they got clever enough to beat us to the sweet corn the night before we were going to harvest it. They've done it every year since. I didn't even bother planting corn this year."

"We gave up on corn too. But not for those reasons," Tony replied, remembering the weak, leggy plants we had grown the previous year. He was definitely not impressed, however, when somebody started making off with our chickens, leaving behind some very raccoon-like tracks. And then Mum told her kits about the sour cherries.

"Hun," I said. "Somebody's playing in the cherry trees. You might want to get out there."

The flashlight revealed five pairs of eyes, masticating jaws and tongues very adept at spitting out pits like peas from a peashooter. Their timing was perfect. Harvest was scheduled for the next day.

I heard the front door slam, running footsteps, a few curses and the trees being shaken. These were Tony's cherries that he had been nursing tenderly since early spring—and they were being eaten right out from under his nose. An emergency trip to Montreal to borrow Joan's live-trap was in order.

"Let me show you how it works," she cautioned. "It has a few quirks."

By the time he remembered the quirks and figured out how to actually set it, the cherries were long gone and the point was moot. That year, our total harvest from a dozen cherry trees was one pathetic basket. Tony doesn't encourage the raccoons any more.

❧ ❦ ❧ ❦ ❧ ❦ ❧ ❦

So the principle that took us so long to learn is that by the time we realize our harvest is compromised, it's long been eaten.

suckers for punishment

By the end of winter, we'd simply had enough of the wind whistling through our hair in the living room—with the windows closed. It, and the adjacent study, became the next plan of attack in our home renovation learning curve.

The living room, particularly, was terrible. It had the same worn brown carpet we had so gladly torn out of the kitchen, only here we'd had to cut a large corner out of it where Squirtie had peed entire lakes when we first moved in and the smell had lingered as only such unpleasant ones do. This had exposed the nauseating lemon yellow and lime coloured linoleum. Peeling beige wallpaper adorned the walls (I swear beige and brown must have been the Chartrands' favourite colours!) and the woodstove sat in a corner surrounded by decorative brick glued to a buckling heat shield.

The study *looked* reasonable. White wallpaper speckled with sunflowers covered the sheets of panelling, and the thick, wide pine floorboards—even if they were painted, guess what, chocolate brown—were cupped but salvageable.

Tony went to fetch his favourite renovation tool: the crowbar.

"Whatever we do," he said. "It won't be worse than it is now."

Arms above his head, he arched his back and swung the crowbar forward like an upside-down pendulum. It landed with a dull thud in the carpet. The effect was negligible, but a wave of accomplishment rushed through him.

Within the hour, the wretched carpet, followed by layers of lino, long-defunct agricultural newspaper, plywood sub floor and something that looked like tar paper metamorphosed from a flat walking surface into a mighty mountain in the centre of the room. As though somebody had pulled upwards from a string in the middle. The net gain was almost an inch. Very encouraging.

"Betcha there's fifteen layers of crap on the walls and ceiling too," mused Tony prophetically.

Indeed there were.

"Ooh, look," he said, eyed glued to the 1974 Playboy centrefold found between two layers of panelling. "The hairstyles were quite different back then."

"Uh-hm," I replied absently, eyes equally glued to the afro hairstyle of an extremely well endowed Playgirl centrefold. "There's something for everyone in these walls. How very thoughtful. Any idea what this might have been for?" I continued, tweezering out barley grains and a passage from the Bible from deep inside a brass bed knob.

As the last layer of panelling caved from the blow struck by the crowbar, it released a torrent of granular insulation that poured out of the hole like a waterfall until it reached our knees. That and the mountain of rubble in the middle of the room now filled it completely.

"Tony," I whimpered from the other side of the mountain. "I'm boxed in."

"Well, let's not stop now," he replied. "Just toss the plaster and lathe out of the window. We can put it on the burning pile later. It'll save a step."

The one step it did save was replaced by about four it did not. Much to our chagrin, the rain shower that ensued cemented the plaster to the grass, and clean up became quite an ordeal.

Tony swore. He swore a lot when he was stressed. I remembered one time, early in our relationship when we were still living in Montreal, he had phoned me at McGill. The conversation began not with "Hello" or "It's me," but with a string of bright blue epithets. It had taken me a while to elicit from him that he had locked himself out of the Mazda with the engine running, and pleeeze could I get the spare key from home and meet him before the car ran out of gas and the engine burned up. Then, as now, the choice of vernacular was justified.

"The studs aren't evenly spaced," he said in amazement, after the room had been cleared. "And look—some of them are even sideways. They'll have to be shimmed. You know what this all means."

I did not, but I found out very soon. And what I found was not to my liking.

It meant that the standard sheets of drywall, which are a breeze to install in a modern house, had to be cut into bizarre shapes to accommodate the spacing. To add insult to injury, we were unable to rent a hoist to hold those lead-heavy sheets on the ceiling.

"We'll have to do it the hard way," said Tony.

The hard way was for me to shinny up a stepladder with one end of the sheet resting on my back and position it while Tony balanced the other end on his head as he sunk in a few strategic screws. By the time both ceilings were done, all trace of good humour had, like Elvis, long since left the building.

We did, however, like the idea of marking our passage in the house. Pierre Trudeau had left this world for another the week before and the newspapers were full of retrospectives, some flattering, others less so. The *National Post* section on his funeral seemed particularly appropriate to insert into walls that had almost killed us.

"I have an idea," Tony chewed at me across the dining table one evening. "I'm sick of being cold in the kitchen. I know how to fix it."

"What does this have to do with renovating the living room at the other end of the house, sweetie?" I asked.

"I'm going to install a vent and fans up there," he replied, pointing across the house to the corner above the wood stove with a vegetable curry-laden knife. "Then run piping down the wall, along the basement ceiling and back up into the kitchen." The vegetable curry deserted the knife and followed a similar trace along the dining room floor.

"Well then, now's the time," I replied, my eyes also following that trace with a mental wet rag.

We had just discovered that the wood stove needed to be replaced, so I wasn't worried about a few extra dollars' worth of piping. Contrary to our insurance papers indicating that it was correctly installed—clearly, nobody had ever bothered to check—it wasn't. A beast of that vintage should have been sixty centimetres away from any walls. In our living room, that meant across a doorway and a quarter of the way into the room. Hence the need for a sexy new stove with a wall clearance of only ten centimetres and no need for a heat shield.

The floorboards morphed from crippled ugly ducklings into swans in an event reminiscent of a sand storm. When it eventually landed, the sawdust amounted to six garbage bags, and that's not counting what we vacuumed, swallowed, shook from our clothes and swept off the walls. It was the second clean-up ordeal within a few months, made only slightly less distressing thanks to the glimmer of light at the end of the tunnel.

The rooms are beautiful and warm now, and our urge to renovate elsewhere has temporarily evaporated. It's time to put our feet up on the sofa, watch the flames dancing in the stove, strawberry daiquiri in hand, and look back in amazement.

only mad dogs and englishmen go out in the midday sun

If the drought of 1999 was bad, the drought of 2001 was far worse. Eight straight weeks without a drop of rain. Tony, the self-appointed waterer, spent a good part of those eight weeks getting intimately acquainted with our irrigation system—the garden hose. Two hours, hose in hand, every other day still weren't enough to get a good crop out of such thirsty plants as watermelon and cantaloupe. They were small but delicious—and only ripe in September, marginally before the first frosts. Even foolproof tomatoes, happy to grow in just about any conditions, suffered and two-thirds of the crop developed blossom-end rot and went straight into the compost. My heart went out to every farmer.

In addition to the drought, a brutal stretch of temperatures in the thirty-five degree range and a humidex of forty-six degrees didn't help matters any. As wells dried up, people wept bitter tears over their beautiful lawns-gone-brown. Instead of rejoicing over the free time they gained from not having to mow, withdrawal symptoms took over and they mowed the desiccated stems instead. Canada's reputation as a winter playground was in jeopardy. I felt terribly sorry for any animals with inadequate shade, heads hanging low, drinking warm mud from dry watering holes. The meltwater pond in the southwest field dried up and cracked. In spite of the plentiful spring-fed ponds, the slower-moving wildlife was having a hard time quenching its collective thirst. Water was definitely a "hot" issue.

The unfamiliar prints in the bottom of the chickens' water pan one morning, the general mess and the hole in the fence confirmed my sneaking suspicion that we were watering some nocturnal wildlife. Whoever those raccoons were, they drank there all summer and we repaired the fence with monotonous regularity until it took on the appearance of a patchwork quilt.

Matt's menagerie spent the summer on our lawn. We left a sympathy bowl of water out for them one day since they refused to go home. Within a week, we found ourselves leaving two enormous pans of water out every day simply to accommodate demand. The ducks, bunny and chickens drank thirstily and noisily but still not enough to consume two pans. We finally gained some insight on the disappearing water when we found a duck "swimming" in each pan. The number of ducks being greater than the number of pans, demand ran high. When one duck had overstayed his turn, another would squeeze his way in and pop the first one out. Why they preferred our pans to the splash pool Matt set up for them remains a mystery.

Tony's watering activities fascinated the ducks and they pestered him no end. No sooner than the first squirt hit them, his clever idea of spraying them homeward had quite the opposite effect. They turned quacking into the spray, smiled, closed their eyes with evident pleasure and asked why on earth they should go home when there was room service here.

Rain eventually came in the form of violent storms. The relief from the crushing heat was indescribable. I now understand the celebrations in India when the monsoons arrive. Only it monsooned here, too. The parched earth couldn't possibly absorb this volume of water and the low areas quickly flooded. I harvested the remains of the broccoli in what could easily pass for a rice-paddy and swam back to the kitchen.

Whoever's doing the rain dance," I thought to myself, "can stop now."

neither a lender nor a borrower be

Before Matt bought the barn across the road, it stood unused for many years, slowly acquiring that lived-in yet worn-out look. Junk filled it all the way up the walls; that very same junk being treasure of immeasurable value to aficionados of garage sales, country auctions and bargains in general. The door was unlocked. We caved to temptation.

Among the goodies, we found this humungous window, in excellent condition, double-glazed and perfect for the porch. We had to have it! Tony and I opened the barn door wide, looked left and right to check for oncoming traffic and potential witnesses. Nothing. Perfect.

"That's it. Stop! NOW!" I cried.

I dropped my end with a thunk in the middle of the road sooner than I'd have liked. On its corner too, which can't have done it any good. As I massaged my aching fingers, a trundling noise approached. We turned our heads, expecting to be eyeball to headlight with a pickup. Roger, bless his cotton socks and plaid shirt, was bringing his very sturdy dolly.

"Saw you having a bit of a time," he boomed in our ears. "Thought I could give you a hand."

"Thanks, Roger," yelled back Tony. "That's very neighbourly of you." He gulped, reddening slightly as he saw the barn door still open, rocking gently on its hinges. Roger and George Vanderveen, the owner of the barn—the very same man who had forgotten where his own septic tank was laid—were still in touch. The fact that Vanderveen had moved to Brockville after severing the farmhouse from the barn wouldn't help should he choose to slap a breaking-and-entering charge on us.

That evening, I felt morally obliged to make a pre-emptive call to ask if he might be willing to sell us a window we had seen in the barn. Not realizing which one I meant or not wanting to bother, and clearly uninterested as to how we had actually clapped eyes on it—it was ours, he said. Honour was saved by a whisker.

෴ ෴ ෴ ෴ ෴ ෴ ෴ ෴

After Matt bought the barn and ramped up his horse business, most of the junk found a new home at the municipal dump and the barn filled with hay instead. His need to feed all those hungry mouths in winter increased equivalently. Why one of those monster round bales spent two winters lying in the ditch in front of the barn I'm not sure, but that's exactly what it did. As feed, it was now useless. As mulch for *our* garden, it was perfect, especially since we were running a little short.

We carefully planned Operation Step 'n Fetch for a time of day when Matt wasn't usually around to do chores. Into the ditch we hopped, hauling armfuls of hay into the wheelbarrow and leaving a trail of evidence behind us. Matt's truck approached as I was wheeling the last barrow-load across the road.

"Get outta the ditch," I yelled to Tony, who, in the rustle of hay, didn't hear a thing.

A total yellow coward, I abandoned my partner in crime and scuttled away, head low in utter shame, trying to look as though I'd come from elsewhere. Out of one eye, I could see Tony leaning nonchalantly on what was left of the bale and Matt, hands on hips at the edge of the ditch, looking down at him. Has anybody ever been caught in such *flagrante delicto*?

"Yeah," Tony said, in answer to my question, back in the garden. "He was a bit surprised to see me in there."

"I'll say," I replied. "What was your excuse?"

"The straight truth," he said, his freckles slowly returning to their customary colour. Tony is about as good a liar as I am. "There was nowhere else to go. He seemed okay with it." Once again, honour was saved.

ಎ ೡ ೪ ೬ ೩ ೡ ೪ ೬

Thanks to the raccoons, Matt's little Rhode Island Red rooster was now the sole survivor of that batch of birds. In his solitude, he was dead keen to hang out with our girls. He spent entire days outside our run, squawking at them, gazing longingly at them through the fencing. He wore out a patch of grass, he wanted to belong so badly. Since the girls were not laying well at the moment, I doubted Tony would want to add a non egg-producing bird to the flock and another mouth to feed on organic mash. I was wrong. In a moment of weakness, he opened the door to the enclosure, shooed the rooster in and slammed it shut again.

"He'll be safe now," he said firmly. And that was that. Matt never even noticed. No need to save honour this time. Besides, we had so little left at this point.

standoff at the harvest moon corral

Where there is a combination of chicken feed, water and shelter, it follows that there will be rats. We've resigned ourselves to the idea. God bless our cats, the next item up on that particular food chain. In spite of all the goodwill and cunning hunting skills in the world, however, they can't keep up with the constant procreation. The surviving rodents are bold, wily and act like the coop belongs to them.

On turning the corner into the run, we sometimes surprise a few as they scurry back to the safety of a hole. If we keep very still, a twitchy, whiskery nose will reappear, checking to see if it's safe and predator-free.

This time was different.

There was the usual scattering when Tony rounded the corner, but one, the king of the pack, didn't move. He sat on his haunches, front paws tucked into his chest, finishing a crumb of corn in his own sweet time.

"Holy cow," muttered Tony. "This one's enormous."

For a split second, neither of them knew what to do next. Tony reacted first. He stamped his foot. Nothing. King Rat stared stonily back at him, although he did deign to stop chewing. Tony stamped his foot again, harder, raising a puff of corn dust. No reaction.

"Buggered if I'm going to be beaten by a rat," thought Tony, whose florid imagination picked this very moment to play back all those horror movies in which rats occupy a starring role. The thought of this cocky rodent clawing its way quickly up his trouser-leg, under his shirt and attaching itself firmly to his face sent a rather large tingle up his spine and back down again. Tony froze, trapped by his thoughts. Snapping back to reality, he jumped up and down like a kid on a trampoline, shouting and waving his arms like a windmill in a tornado.

Whatever thoughts the rat had about finding a diplomatic solution to the standoff evaporated. This would be a *mano-a-mano* combat. A fight to the very end. For justice. For glory.

Tony mentally prepared himself for a similar combat. He ripped from his mind the picture of a white underbelly clinging to his nose and a rather large pair of *cohones* dangling somewhere in the vicinity of his mouth. Ugh! His resolve wavered… No, he needed to focus! Would this be a dignified pistols-at-dawn contest or a downright dirty, rolling-in-the-chicken-shit affair? As if expecting a Sumo wrestler to appear, he hunkered down in battle-ready position, ears straining for a clue, and waited…

Blinking through a veritable mushroom cloud of corn dust, Tony surveyed the result of his efforts. The chickens had vanished. So had the rat.

Score—rat, zero; Tony, "won."

don't put all your eggs in one basket

"You go get the eggs," muttered Tony sleepily.

"No, you go," I whined.

"I went all week. It's your turn," he replied firmly. Not a morning man if he can help it, my husband.

And with that, the discussion closed. Neither of us took any pleasure in winter egg collection. Going early enough to prevent them from freezing meant getting out of a warm bed to face the elements.

He rolled over, wrapping the duvet around him as he went—yet to open his eyes.

"Fine!" I was wide awake now. Uncovered, my head-to-toe night regalia wasn't keeping me nearly warm enough.

I pulled a toque down to my eyebrows, slipped a neck tube over it far enough to only expose my eyes, pushed up the hood of my nightrobe, put my barn coat over the whole outfit and added the finishing touches to this "have-you-looked-in-the-mirror-recently?" outfit with barn boots and mittens. The Michelin Man had nothing on me.

The path painstakingly shovelled through the deep snow to the coop had disappeared—again!—in snowdrifts accumulated by the prevailing west wind. Over night, freezing rain had formed an icy crust over the entire outside world. The trees dripped icicles long enough to use in a sword-fight. In spite of the fresh, blue sky, it was an unfriendly morning. In the stillness of the morning air, only the rooster belted his lungs out.

"Oh, shut up!" I muttered irritably, sinking up to my thighs with each crunchy step. The cold snow penetrated between my pyjamas and my boots and melted its way to my ankles. I rounded the corner to the coop on an ice-patch, dancer-like, on one foot. The chickens were laying well in spite of their meagre surroundings.

"You are such good girls," I told them, with a light pat on the back each.

They cooed softly as I reached under them and filled the basket with perfectly formed brown eggs. I slipped one into each mitt to keep my hands warm.

The return trip was even harder. Ice-crystals formed on my eyelashes, bonding upper and lower eyelids together. I aimed for the sinkholes my footsteps had already made but somehow my stride no longer fit. I struggled to keep my balance in all these wretched layers. Without warning and certainly without time to cry out, my body performed a manoeuvre I couldn't repeat if I tried. I found myself upside down, arms spread wide, feet pedalling in the air, having broken through a crust of ice with my face. It was as though someone had shoved a Cabbage Patch doll into the snow head first. Graceful it was not.

"The eggs!" I thought, in a panic.

My first concern was for those in my mitts. My fingers groped tentatively for slimy albumen inside what should have been a warm refuge for my hands. I thanked my lucky stars and tried not to think of the mess that might have been. In that nano-second of commotion, I had had the presence of mind to save the eggs at the expense of my face. I extracted myself from the snow bank and wiped myself on a sleeve of dubious cleanliness. My nose was cut and bleeding, and I anticipated two owlish black eyes to return to McGill with next day. Unwillingly, I admired the subconscious reaction that had cast self-preservation aside in favour of trade goods. I picked up my pride and the basket and searched, through puffy eyelids, for signs of omelette *à la* snow. No eggs had even fallen out. Mission accomplished.

Actually, mission not-quite-so-accomplished. Once my eyelashes had melted in the relative warmth of the kitchen, I could see that seven of them bore an impressive spread of cracks. We would have to eat them ourselves.

Still somewhat damp, I climbed back into bed, snuggled up tightly against Tony and contemplated how many eggy meals I could possibly make him eat in a row without rebellion.

chickadee circus

"Have you tried to tame chickadees?" Peter Kuhns, McGill buddy and bird-watcher extraordinaire, asked in response to my story.

I had just told him about our weekend, skiing at the Upper Canada Migratory Bird Sanctuary. Coming through a well-worn trail at the edge of the woods, Tony had been ambushed by a veritable flock of chickadees.

"Tony," I laughed. "They're flying around your head just like in the cartoons when someone has a concussion." I longed for a camera. Two of them landed on his head, still chickadee-dee-deeing. Proof that life really can mimic animation.

Under any other circumstances, I might have mocked Peter. Taming chickadees indeed! But this had been so surprising that I was ready to accept anything.

"No, I haven't," I replied. "What should I do?" I didn't think Tony would approve of playing with wild birds instead of doing something more constructive, so I wasn't expecting to spend much time at this.

"Easy. Stand by your feeder, very still, one arm outstretched, with a good load of sunflower seeds in your palm. Chickadees are extremely intelligent and just asking to be friendly. They'll land readily on your arms. They have a well-developed frontal lobe, so unlike squirrels, they store their seed *and* remember where they put it."

Opened after the Seaway was constructed in the Fifties to preserve a pristine, nine thousand hectare site made up of marshy wetlands and maple bush, the Sanctuary attracts as many bird-watchers as it does Canada geese. The chickadees there must have learned this trick very quickly. And I had learned not to doubt Peter in anything, so I applied their principle and stored the information for later use.

A few winters later, Anne-Marie Blythe and Fiona Rennig, two former McGill colleagues, came to visit. A perfect opportunity to give them a day to remember. Off to the Sanctuary we went, in spite of the frigid temperature, the howling wind and their inadequate footwear. The road into what is now the sanctuary used to lead to Aultsville village in the days before the Seaway. Apparently, when the water level on this side of the Cornwall dam is low, the foundations of the homes that were razed to the ground in the name of progress poke through the roots of the bulrushes in a spooky memory of lives once lived and torn apart. In terms of our visit, the trees bordering the old road offered some protection from the elements and a convenient place to park not far from the anticipated action.

"Put some seed in the brim of your hat," I suggested to Fiona. "And keep very still."

"Oh, this is a great photo opp," said Anne-Marie, excitedly getting into position with her camera. "Don't move."

"I'm not about to," replied Fiona from tight, unmoving jaws. I wasn't sure if they were clenched from the biting cold that had turned her nose into a running faucet or because a chickadee had already swooped, landed on her hat and immediately flown off with a seed.

"Ohhhhh. Missed that. I'm pretty sure I've just taken a shot of your eyes and hat, but no bird."

"Okay. Bring some more seed. Let's set it up again," said Fiona, in a fit of giggles. "This is too good to miss and nobody will believe me without photo evidence."

"Shhhh. They'll never come back." Anne-Marie positioned herself again. "Hold it right there... Steady... Ohhhhhhh... Missed again"

Peals of laughter rang out. Fiona stamped her feet in her thin boots and sniffed loudly.

"Hurry up. Soon, they won't want to land because I'll be shivering so much."

"No kidding!" In spite of the cute little fingerless gloves she was wearing that were now topped with stiff, blue-ish fingers, Anne-Marie could barely contain her laughter. "My hands are going to freeze to the camera soon anyway."

"I'm ready"

"Me too." Anne-Marie took a deep breath to steady herself and suppress the giggles. "Ohhhhhh..."

"It's too cold. That's it. I'm done!" said Fiona in a combination of frustration and laughter.

She emptied the brim of her hat onto the snow as we reached the car. The chickadees swarmed down.

Anne-Marie, seeing this out of the corner of her eye, spun around.

"I can get that," she cried, raising the camera to her eye. "Ohhhh..."

The chickadees fluttered off, determined never to have their antics captured on film.

Some months later, Anne-Marie showed me the snaps she had taken that day. Fiona's hat featured prominently. There wasn't a chickadee in sight. In spite of having an excellent eye for landscapes, I cautioned that she would never make a living as a photographer for the *National Geographic*.

sun today, snow tomorrow, job the day after

The farm cannot continue. Tony sat down and calculated our profits from the previous year's hard labour. We made a life-sucking $1.75 an hour—each, mind you. It's all well and good to see grocery stores bursting with food as long at the people on the inside of the farm gate, here and even more so abroad, make a decent living at it. No wonder people prefer sit-down jobs.

The clincher turned out to be the unpredictable weather, on top of our financial "challenges." Anybody depending on the elements for a living at the turn of the twenty-first century is on the endangered list; from ski-hill operators to retail outlets selling lawn mowers, snowmobiles and bikinis. Farmers, to whom a few weeks of drought or rain at the wrong time can make a world of difference in harvest quantity and quality, are right in the line of fire.

That year, summer existed in name only. This time, there was no Mount Pinatubo to blame. Environment Canada declared that there had been almost a hundred and fifty fewer hours of sun than normal. Grumpy, pasty-looking citizens wondered if we truly needed to pay such high taxes to a government that announced the glaringly obvious.

By mid-July, we needed to make a decision about the rest of the season. Spring crops such as peas and lettuce hadn't done well, sitting as they were up to their elbows in mud. A full harvest of the already-delayed summer vegetables would be further compromised if the first frost appeared on time in mid-September.

So we cancelled the season. It seemed only fair to refund our sharers' money, minus the cost of seed. They had only seen a few, poor leaves of lettuce for their money. We had seen even less for our efforts. We told the sharers they could call us on an occasional basis (assuming that we might harvest more than a total zero), ask what was available that week and pay for it on a cash-and-carry basis if they were interested.

Tony and I faced a loss of several thousand dollars instead of the means with which to build the garage/workshop and pay the bills for the money-guzzling Jetta.

Over the winter, we discussed the extreme weather trends we had experienced both over the past couple of years and over the decade. We discussed changing from community-supported agriculture to another method; from field vegetables to greenhouse; from elbow grease to mechanization. We discussed survival without a small but regular farm income. We discussed the transition of the organic movement from that of a niche market for the small farmer to its hijacking by corporate farms supplying grocery chains and the subsequent fall in prices. The conclusions were the same. Harvest Moon Farm, producer of quality organic vegetables, is as dead as our dreams of giving up the rat race. On a larger scale, food production in North America must adapt to reflect the changes it cannot control. Welcome to globalization.

The time had come for me to actually live on the premises with Tony and give up the crazy commute to Montreal, to start climbing the greasy pole again. I will commute daily to Ottawa instead with either Katrina, Dan's wife, or with Kristen Stoddard's group from Ingleside—the official local carpool. We will keep the chickens and reduce the garden to a manageable size—plant for ourselves, the freezer, friends and family who appreciate quality food. The stress from the lack of harvest will be replaced by the fun and satisfaction of gardening.

Farmers we ain't no more.

*the climbin'-the-corporate-
ladder-again years*

getting there is half the battle

"Oh, sorry!" whispered Anne-Marie apologetically in response to my grunt down the phone. "I forgot about the time difference."

Recently back from her own Best Coast adventures, she had agreed to house- and cat-sit during our week in Kelowna. I was at a conference; Tony was enjoying a pre-Christmas vacation.

"But I *had* to call," she continued. "Someone left a voicemail for you. They want to interview you right away."

Instead of leaping, my heart sank. I needed to figure out *prontissimo* what physicists have been working on since time began—how to be in two places at once.

"And… Squirtie-cat got out. I opened the back door to get firewood and a black streak shot past me. She's the only one who moves that fast."

This was a much greater concern. The Squirt was unlikely to be coaxed back inside by a stranger, and Eastern Ontario was in the grip of a record-breaking cold snap.

"Okay," I replied. "First things first. Leave the porch door open, put some food and a couple of blankets out there. We'll get the Squirt in when we come home. In the meantime, at least she'll have shelter. Now, give me the phone number of this company. I'll do my best to make nice."

Wide awake now, I called immediately and booked the very last available interview slot—nine o'clock on the morning of our return. This would be tight.

"We need a strategy," said Tony, when I updated him.

"You bet," I agreed.

"Well, it's actually very simple…"

I've learned from bitter experience that whatever should be simple never is, and whatever isn't always lives up to its reputation. There were two strikes against us right from the get-go.

"…We left the car at Ben and Maggie's in Ottawa, and we'll be sleeping there before driving back to Ingleside. Why don't I just drop you off at the interview on the way home and I'll wait for you."

It did sound easy. I was immediately sceptical.

Airline schedules and airport security being what they are these days, we had no expectation of our flight home landing on time. We were right. And since we were also well beyond the hour at which there is a living soul left at Ottawa's modest airport, hailing a taxi required a couple of phone calls to some very reluctant cab companies. The temperature may have been a factor that particular night. It was minus twenty-three degrees Celsius a whole thirty degrees colder than where we were a few short hours ago. We sat on our suitcases, shivering and yawning at the same time.

Our dear friends, Ben and Maggie, realized we were *non compos mentis* and packed us straight off to bed. I paused long enough to rinse out a pair of undies for the next day. I do have some standards.

When the alarm assaulted us the following morning, I regretted not taking my contacts out or brushing my teeth. Maybe a thick coat of make-up would brighten my face enough that I could pull the wool over the interviewer's eyes. In the meantime, Tony went to scrape the windshield and start the car. The thermometer in the kitchen window was stuck in the same position as when we arrived and the wind had picked up. The forecast wasn't optimistic.

"Forget it," he said, blown back inside by the cold. "All the doors are frozen shut. I had to climb in through the trunk." This was another of the Jetta's quirks. We were no strangers to entering our car—in the most public of places—via the trunk, through the central arm rest in the back seat and *voilà*. As the skinny lightweight, that task usually fell to me. So far, nobody had called the cops on us.

"Oh yes," replied Ben evenly from behind the *Ottawa Citizen*. "We had freezing rain a couple of nights ago. That would have done the trick."

"That, the flat tire and the flat battery," continued Tony, warming his cold, stiff hands on a mug of coffee.

"Ah."

"I'll call CAA to get a boost and put the spare on while I'm waiting. Sylviane…" he turned to me "…forget the interview."

"Interview? What interview?" questioned Ben. He put both his toast and the newspaper down.

"I have, sorry—had—an interview this morning. I'll call to cancel."

Ben whipped himself up into high gear and reached for the phone.

"I'm working today," he said. "So I can't take you. Let me call a neighbour."

"You really think your neighbour wants a specimen like me in his car?" I began. We had carefully wrapped our Okanagan ice wine in many layers of clothing and packed it tightly in the suitcase. In that very same clothing, I now looked like a crumpled piece of tissue paper.

"You'll fit right in," he replied brightly.

Josh pulled up in a spiffy-looking BMW. He, on the other hand, looked as though Ben had pulled him right out of bed. Under his toque and down coat, I'm sure he was still in his pyjamas. Certainly, he'd had no time to shave. I both apologized and thanked him profusely.

"Wait for me if I'm not there," called Tony as the Bimmer scrunched over the ice and out of the driveway. "CAA says everybody needs a boost this morning. This could take a while."

So far, nothing had gone right. How much worse could it get?

"What are the elements of a good quote?" asked the interviewer.

My mind went blank. I looked at him through gritty contact lenses that made my eyes water. My undies were still damp enough to feel cold and clammy. I squirmed uncomfortably in my chair and uttered a feeble reply that set the tone for the rest of the meeting.

"Do you make allowances for jet-lag?" I asked at the end of the interminable hour, half of which had been a written grammar test. "I could really use it."

One of these days, I might just learn to pick the battles I can win.

if the shoe fits, don't throw it away

"I'm calling from the *Yellowknifer* newspaper," said the voice at the other end of the line. Puzzled at being called over two weeks after the signing ceremony and meetings, I put my mind into reverse gear. "No, no," she insisted. "It's not about that. Somebody found your shoe."

To backtrack…

The Royal Architectural Institute of Canada, for which I had recently started working, and the provincial architectural associations held meetings in Yellowknife in November 2001, to sign the Reciprocity Agreement with the NWT Association of Architects. A fine banquet was held in the Legislative Assembly on the Saturday evening to celebrate the occasion.

Exhausted after two days of hard meetings, my colleague, Veronica, and I decided to walk back to the hotel for some extremely fresh air via a snowmobile trail shortcut over Frame Lake, behind the Visitors' Centre. It was about minus thirty-five degrees Celsius.

Suddenly, I heard an anguished cry behind me. Veronica had fallen through the ice. I heard another cry. It was mine—like an out-of-body experience, except the frigid water leaching through my clothes was a brisk reminder that my body and I were definitely one and the same. Somehow, Veronica managed to crash her way ahead of me and instead of doing the sensible thing—retracing our footsteps—we found ourselves stumbling forward through the frozen muck and ice until we hit dry land again.

"Oh no!" I cried.

"What?" replied Veronica, fearing the worst as we examined ourselves for injury. "Are you frostbitten? Hypothermic? Are your legs numb?"

"I've lost one of my dress shoes," I wailed, once again putting material goods ahead of personal safety. "It must have fallen out of my pocket in that mess back there."

It was close to midnight, each boot contained more icy water than a champagne bucket and my pants had frozen to my legs, so I wasn't about to stick around and look. Big mistake.

"What am I going to do with *one* shoe?" I wailed to Veronica, as we ran back to the hotel as best our frozen, sodden clothes would allow. "Not only are they beautiful, soft Italian leather pumps that fit like a glove, but they have lots of sentimental value. I paid three dollars for them at the Salvation Army in Montreal. No tax." I was devastated.

Next morning, I examined the site closely. With hindsight and in the clear light of day, I would never have taken that trail. The ice was quite obviously thinner than elsewhere. Since I was leaving the following morning, approaching the exact spot was a no-no. I didn't feel like showing up at the airport barefoot if something happened to my only remaining boots. I was about to give the shoe up for dead when a dog-walker approached. The light bulb went on in my head.

"Do you think your dog might sniff around and retrieve my shoe?" I asked politely.

"I doubt it," she answered. "He's not that bright." To my horror and despite my warnings, she walked right over the thin ice to where I was pointing.

"Don't worry," she said, seeing the look on my face. She bounced up and down, "I walk here all the time."

Crack! Guess what.

"Oh dear," she continued ruefully, climbing out of the hole, "I've just pushed your shoe in."

I resigned myself to never wearing my very favourite shoes again. Back at the hotel and ready to pack, I debated the odds of it being found or even if it would be wearable. I made a heartbreaking decision. With many misgivings, I put the orphan shoe in the trash in favour of northern souvenirs.

Unknown to me, but obviously filled with Catholic-sized guilt, the lady returned—more adequately dressed in hip waders—and groped around in the slush until she found it. An ad appeared in the *Yellowknifer* a few days after I left town. The paper received so many calls about the shoe (I didn't realize I had whined all over town) that it ran a Cinderella article. The Visitors' Centre, where I had left my name and number should it ever surface, gave my contact details to the journalist. And that's how she got in touch with me.

So now that the left one has been found, and my grateful thanks to Denise Blundell for her tenacity, two questions remain. Is it wearable? If so, I shall just have to weep. And, further to the challenge put out by Arthur Black on CBC's *Basic Black* a few weeks later when he read this story on the air, are there any volunteers to go to the Yellowknife dump to retrieve the other one?

déjà-vu all over again

The sight that greeted me at the far end of the driveway reminded me of scenes of London after the Blitz: thin chimneys of smoke rising into the breeze, charred beams standing at attention like skeletons, broken glass, melted plastic, rubble, rubble and more rubble…

I stared in disbelief. This used to be our barn.

"It's all my fault," Tony wept, hands white-knuckling the steering wheel. When the weather is fine, I bike to and from Ingleside to meet Kristen Stoddard's carpool to Ottawa. That day, he had thought it wise to pick me up so he could break the news gently.

I climbed out of the car to get a better perspective—dazed into thinking that, without a windshield to obstruct my view, something might improve.

"What do you mean?"

"I had a feeling somebody was at the door," Tony continued, ignoring my question. "That's the first thing I knew."

Indeed, Roger had been beating so hard on the front door his knuckles were bruised.

"Are you bloody deaf?" he yelled at his normal volume when Tony appeared. "I've been knocking for ten minutes. I phoned but there was no answer and I could see the car so I knew you were home so I walked over..."

He paused long enough to take a breath. Roger no longer walks well so he had actually biked from next door, but that wasn't the point. Even thought he could hear Roger perfectly well with them in, Tony took his earplugs out to be polite.

"I was using power tools upstairs," he replied, whispering in comparison. "Didn't hear a thing. What's up?"

"Your barn's on fire."

Now he had Tony's undivided attention. Roger flattened himself against the door as much as his belly would allow, as Tony barrelled past him and straight to the barn to see for himself. Halfway there, he had all the information he needed. The barn was engulfed in flames. He spun round to fetch the garden hose from the tool shed and ran back with it as far as it would go. Not far enough. For an instant... panic! What now? The chickens! He dropped the useless hose and headed for the run where they had been enjoying a reprieve from the cold on one of spring's first above-zero days. Nobody in sight. So where were they? Huddled in the back corner of the coop—where they thought they were safe!

Tony dashed around the corner to the coop and ducked under the cloud of terrible, black smoke. The bitterness made him cough. Flamelets, like St. Elmo's fire, flickered on the straw at his feet. Raging fireballs above his head brought a beam crashing down. The girls were so, so close but he couldn't reach them without compromising his own safety. Decision time. He froze like a doe in headlights while his brain processed the situation... then resumed his panic.

"So the chickens are dead," Tony gulped through his tears. "The poor rooster only got to live another year after the raccoon incident and he still had a violent end."

In another Olympic sprint, he raced back to the house to call 9-1-1. Had he known the fire truck would take a whopping eighteen minutes to show up, he might not have wasted his breath.

When they finally arrived, the two fire trucks belched a stream of volunteer fire fighters whose dream it must be to play with water and axes. The took it upon themselves to break all the windows we had been collecting to build a greenhouse—even though they were not in the line of fire, so to speak—scatter the compost pile to the four corners of the property after peppering it with broken glass, and bring down the rest of the beams before drowning them with floods of water.

"I could have done that," sniffed Tony bitterly. "Look at that mess. Now we have a huge clean up job."

I felt it wasn't the time to remind him that our own hose had proved inadequate and that he was an expert mess-maker himself.

Later, under cross-examination, Tony admitted to emptying ashes from the wood stove on the compost pile. Apparently, the lesson had not been learned well enough the first time. The fierce west wind that day had rolled some embers under the barn door where they came to rest against the straw set aside for the chickens' nesting boxes. The bale caught like gasoline. Flames licked at the coop—the very same coop we had thickly insulated with straw—and it was all downhill from there. Had we chosen to use them more wisely, those ancient boards of original-growth timber would have made amazing firewood. Instead, they had burned with an intensity that can only be produced by a fire completely out of control.

The girls are dead. The barn is gone. Not much left to call a farm now!

the paradox

The countryside is devoid of pedestrians. Our neighbours visit by car and I see them drive to and fro within the limits of their own property lines, albeit large properties. A pedestrian—any pedestrian—is worth a whole slew of points just for the scarcity factor.

I, on the other hand, love to walk. When we lived in Montreal, I used to trek the eight-kilometre round trip to McGill in all sorts of weather. It gave me thinking time and created a buffer between work stress and home life. Very therapeutic.

On the days that I travel with Katrina, I leave the house early enough that I walk the three kilometres to her house before the two of us head to Ottawa. I enjoy cutting my way through the morning mist that hangs like low cloud across the cedar trees along Mel's Lane, an uninhabited, woodsy gravel road. I glimpse the odd deer or raccoon; I monitor the changing seasons; I see the fresh, unbroken snow on the forest canopy; I hear the honking call of Canada geese flying in wobbly formations overhead; and I listen to audio books or the CBC on my Walkman. In the evenings, we're always running late so she drives me all the way home.

In the dead of winter, when I carpool with Kristen and the Ingleside crew, Tony drops me at her house in the morning. On the return trip, she leaves me at the foot of Wales Road so I can have my "daily constitutional." It's dark by then, so I wear a construction vest over my coat and stay well off the road. I pass the house where the owners feed the deer and cross to the other side to avoid disturbing them; I keep a look out for herons in the marshland; I tiptoe quietly past the home with the huge Rottweiler—actually, I pass an average of two dogs per kilometre, most of them big and bitey—and I listen to audio books or the CBC. Walking is still therapeutic.

Often, a car or pickup truck stops at my side. Somebody grunts as they struggle with the window mechanism and then cries, "Wanna lift?"

"No, thanks," I say. "I enjoy the walk."

"Oh yeah?" comes the unbelieving reply. "You going far?"

"Just up the road, really. But you know, if ever you see me out here in a snowstorm or pouring rain, I'll be happy to accept."

"As long as you're okay," comes the voice, uncertainly.

"Yes. Thanks for stopping," I wave goodbye.

This happens so regularly, the conversation is almost a ritual. Even the snow-plow stopped one day. I regret not accepting that one, if only for the bump-and-grind experience. It's charming that people care, and I now have many sidewalk-to-vehicle relationships. Ask me to recognize the occupants, however, and that's another story.

"I can't take you to Wales Road today," said Kristen, one night. "That traffic jam in Ottawa cost us nearly an hour and we should drop Bill off first."

Bill Guindon, one of the carpoolers, fidgeted in his seat and glanced at his watch. He was due to start coaching a hockey game in Winchester round about now. We weren't close to home yet and he had another half an hour drive ahead of him to get there after picking up his equipment. In his anxiety, he had wriggled tiny Holly Stuart into a corner. We'd all be glad to get out of the van that night.

"No problem, Kristen," I replied. I would simply hitch a lift along Highway Two to Wales Road and then walk as usual. I'd hitched twice before and had barely set off with my thumb in the air before somebody stopped.

As I squinted into the oncoming lane at the dearth of headlights, I absently considered that it might take a little longer this time. After all, it was people's dinner hour.

Headlights came and went. I thumbed vigorously. Nothing. I began to walk. More vehicles came, flicked on their brights—the better to see you, my child—and lowered them the instant they passed me. I was not impressed. And unless I wanted to get home at midnight, I'd better pick up the pace too. Under the alternate light of headlights and the moon, I not only thumbed, I waved madly and jumped up and down like a fool. A certain amount of irritation welled up in me. Where *were* all those kind people now that I needed them?

A school bus slowed and turned onto Fothergill Road. Saved! I ran to catch up with it.

"Do you mind taking me just a couple of kilometres up the road?" I asked the driver, as a teenager jumped down.

"Sorry," she said. "Can't. I'd really like to help." The door closed and the bus was gone.

Now there are many times when applying rules to the letter is a good thing. There are also times when common sense should prevail. This should have been one of those times. Clearly, a small, well-spoken woman in a dress coat, carrying a satchel and walking on a country road between Nowhereville and Nowhereburg does not pose an enormous threat to global security or school kids.

The road darkened and I pressed on. I debated knocking on a farm door and begging for a lift but realized I would have to cross the snow-filled ditch dividing Highway Two from Fothergill Road, climb the wire fencing and fight off any number of dogs. All this in city clothes. It wasn't worth the bother. I looked up the road and saw the street lamp shining on the intersection with Wales Road. Another half an hour or so and I'd be home.

A car sped by. "Y'see," I yelled after it. "I didn't need you anyway!" I followed that with a gesture.

It took me an hour and a bit to walk the eight kilometres from Ingleside. I peeled my boots off in the porch. Steam—or was it gratitude?—rose from my feet. Those boots were *not* made for walking, whatever the song might say about them!

I slowly counted my blisters and considered why nobody had stopped. I was clearly visible in their headlights, waving my arms in the universally understood signal for attention and thumbing like a pro.

Did they all really think I was just saying hello?

the mighty bison hunter

"How was *your* weekend?" I asked Katrina as we travelled to Ottawa on a Monday morning. Our freezer, brand new out-of-the-box chainsaw and car exhaust had crapped out within minutes of each other the day before, so I was fairly certain that hers must have been better than mine.

"Oh, Sylviane," she replied wearily, her eyebrows creased into one long zigzag across her forehead. "I'm just about ready to put the For Sale sign up. The bison are gone."

I had a fridge full of slowly decomposing strawberries that I had been unable to freeze and a seriously depleted bank account. This sounded worse.

"Gone?? Whaddaya mean… gone?"

"Well, the five bulls we just bought broke through the fence and the other twelve animals simply followed them out. They're gone!" Her voice reached a quasi-hysterical crescendo on the last few words.

Now I know those bison are worth five thousand dollars each, so a quick bit of mental arithmetic told me that eighty-five thousand dollars was on the run in the back woods—an accident or lawsuit in the making. Indeed, this did not sound like a good weekend.

"The problem is," she continued, "now that they're off our land, anybody has the right to shoot them as wild animals. Some neighbours have seen them and called us, but they've moved off again by the time Dan gets there. And, of course, he's the only human they know so nobody else is about to make them do anything they don't want to."

She paused long enough to glance at the road in front of us. An excellent driver, blessed with eyes in the back of her head, Katrina had warned me on our first drive together that the speed limit was nothing more to her than a number on a sign. Combined with her non-stop chatter, the hour-long trip passed in a very fun fifty minutes.

"Right now, it looks as though we'll have to shoot them all, wherever they are," she continued "But that really is a last resort. After all, it's our entire herd. Plus, it's not that simple. Not only does a vet have to supervise the slaughter, but we'd have to cut a path into the forest—that isn't ours—so that we can haul the carcasses out by truck. And even then, our slaughterhouse doesn't have the capacity to process seventeen mammoth beasts or the freezer space to store them."

Clearly, there was no easy answer.

That evening, Dan appeared at our front door asking to borrow the newly-repaired chainsaw. The man had serious luggage under his eyes, a testament to his third day without sleep. He looked as though he'd been dragged through a hedge backwards, which probably wasn't far from the truth. We assumed the Flansburys had reached the last resort solution.

"Can't stop," he said, flinging it over his shoulder as he staggered with fatigue to his truck. "I have a plan."

In the car the following morning, Katrina updated me.

"Those bison are costing us a fortune." Her use of the present tense told me they were still alive. "They stampeded through a corn field last night, an angry farmer brandishing a shotgun hot on their heels. Dan had to go and make nice with him and we now have to buy the ravaged crop at his full price. He wasn't very accommodating."

"Oh," I said relieved. "At least you can use it as feed when it's ready for harvest."

"Love to," she replied, with some asperity. "You tell me what organic farmers are supposed to do with corn that was sprayed with god-knows-what just hours before the bison went through it. Talk about Murphy's Law."

"Oh," I repeated, several tones lower this time.

Meanwhile, in the faint hope he might be able to coax them back *à la* Pied Piper, Dan was clearing out the brush and furnishing what appeared to be their chosen bedding area with salt licks and corncobs. He whistled their call and listened closely to the stillness of the woods. The silence was broken by the crack of a twig. Moments later, it was followed by the thundering of hooves and the onslaught of seventeen pairs of pointy horns, beady eyes and enough steel-reinforced foreheads to do a lot—an awful lot—of damage to one puny human. Dan broke into a cold sweat. It wasn't meant to happen like this. He was too young and too tired to die. He spun behind a tree, closed his eyes and held his breath. As the shock-wave from the stampede passed through his body, he acknowledged his survival with a sharp release of breath and unscrewed one eyelid to witness seventeen tails disappearing into the bush.

"Okay," he gasped, both eyes wide open. "We won't be doing that again!"

Guy Whiteside, a man with his own enormous herd of cows and an equal amount of common sense, came up with the more practical idea of moving the corral to their bedding area, baiting it and closing the gate when all the bison had stepped inside. Guy was a grizzled, wiry man with the piercing blue eyes so typical of this area. His small, gnarly hands told of many years of hard labour both as a farmer and general contractor. Dan and Katrina blessed every day that he and his wife, Judy, were in their lives as friends, neighbours and babysitters.

The three men—Dan's brother, Jude, provided the extra brawn to move the corral—lay waiting in a nearby ditch as the animals from the main herd trotted slowly into the corral and… straight into Guy's waiting truck. Two of the men leapt out and did a whoop-di-doo; the third, finding himself horizontal for the first time in days, just lay there snoring.

With the majority of the herd back behind reinforced bars, the five instigators lost their urge to face life on the outside and came running home. Dan and Jude quickly dropped a portion of fence to let them in. It was over.

With his eighty-five thousand dollars safely back where it belonged, Dan finally staggered to bed.

fresh as country air

There are both drawbacks and advantages to having a poor sense of smell.

On a beautiful summer morning, on my way to the Ingleside carpool by bike, I made friends with a skunk and we chatted for a few moments before he disappeared into the ditch. I had no reason to believe he'd been vindictive. My mind distantly contemplating the glorious ruby sunrise over the St. Lawrence River as it bordered Highway Two, I wasn't paying nearly enough attention to the road. Maybe Katrina was rubbing off on me. When another scampered crossed the road, I jammed on the brakes and came to a very abrupt stop in front of him. What were the odds of my luck holding? I was wearing one of my best suits.

Kristen sniffed as she opened the van door for me.

"I don't think it's you," she said reassuringly. "The neighbourhood skunk probably sprayed the van."

I thanked her inwardly for being gracious and we firmly implanted that story on Holly and Bill as they climbed in, noses crinkled, faces questioning. Barb, the chatterbox of the group, was stunned into silence.

The smell refused to disperse. Unfair comparisons were made to the four kittens Bill brought in for a colleague a few weeks before. The poor things had so covered themselves in excrement that I insisted we stop at the convenience store in Finch to clean them up. The mess was such that the storeowner tossed us a roll of paper towels and a bucket of water, and refused to have anything more to do with us. By the time the wrigglers were clean enough to travel, we were somewhat nauseous and excessively behind schedule.

Once at work, I did a quick strip in the privacy of my office, put my suit jacket to my face—just like in those sappy laundry soap commercials—and inhaled. Dear Gods! Roadkill was nothing compared to this. It was incredibly bitter and pervasive. I reeled in horror. My jacket had taken a powerful hit, the skirt not so bad. There was no way the jacket and I could cohabit in a windowless office. I flung it into an empty room across the corridor and hoped nobody would notice. Problem number two, however, would be a little harder to solve. I had dressed to the nines for a meeting at the National Arts Centre, where I doubted anyone would take kindly to bumpkins. The jacket was a must to complete the outfit.

"Do you smell skunk?" asked my colleague, Nadia, putting her head around my door. "How can that be, four floors up and downtown?"

"It's me," I replied brightly.

"Phew!" she closed the door, not to return. "And I thought the smog was bad enough."

Ooohs and aaaahs percolated into my lair. The smell and the story spread across the office and down the elevator at the speed unfavourable tales do. I found myself ostracized. Colleagues are one thing, but how could I go to the NAC and appear urbane and credible? I started chain-sucking mentholated cough candies in the hope they would disguise, if not altogether mask, the smell radiating from my person like an aura.

"Hello," Victoria Ionson greeted me at the NAC, nostrils wide.

Here was someone I was keen to impress; someone with a sophisticated mind, a vast store of literary knowledge from which she could quote entire paragraphs, a high-ranking job with an organization I would crawl over hot coals to work for—and a disappointingly good sense of smell. There was nothing for it. I had to confess.

"Oh, you live in the country! I've always wanted to live in the country. It must be wonderful. The birds, the trees, the cows, the fresh country air…"

She was charmed.

"City girl," I thought. But I noticed she stayed up-wind and chose to the open window.

The day dragged on eternally. I suffocated in my little office-box; eyes on the verge of watering. My colleagues sent email instead of visiting. The lonely life of a pencil pusher…

Tony greeted me at the front door with a cheesy grin and the garden hose. News really does travel fast. I eyed the hose askance.

"No, no," he reassured me, reading my mind yet unable to wipe the grin off his face. "I was just about to water the garden."

I grunted in disbelief.

In a now familiar scene, although this time—to the delight of passing traffic—in broad daylight, I stripped in the porch before stepping inside. Anyone would think I was an exhibitionist!

ain't no flies on us!

There are flies in the house. Not in summer, when they abound outside. Nooooo. We have them in winter. All winter. Everywhere. Tony hates them with a passion bordering on obsession. I mostly don't care except when they zing around my head. They do, however, make the best live toy a cat could possibly wish for, as well as a good, crunchy snack.

I can't imagine what cluster flies live on because they're not interested in people-food, and I don't know where they come from. Can't be the deep-freeze outside—so what's left? They hatch in the walls? Surely not. What I do know is that we are not alone.

"We have flies in the house," Tony confided shamefully to Roy at the hardware store in Ingleside. "Got anything?"

Roy led Tony to a prominent, but empty, aisle. There wasn't a thing on the shelves.

"Got anything?" repeated Tony, looking around in disbelief.

"Oh, there was a cold snap a couple of nights ago and the entire village swarmed that aisle and cleaned us out. They took everything from fly-paper to RAID," he replied.

Apparently, Perry knew that indoor cluster flies were no big secret and certainly not unique either. Tony located a lone fly swatter.

"I'll take this," he said. And he didn't let go of it until spring.

I needed a basis for comparison. Since I arrived at Katrina's a little early one morning, I took the opportunity to peek at their kitchen windowsill. The dark hours had left an accumulation worthy of the expression *dropping like flies*. Katrina caught my glance as she emerged. I reddened somewhat.

"You know, once upon a time, we considered getting an iguana to… uhm… lick the problem," she said, needing no explanation for my actions.

I laughed. Tony and I had had the same idea, but on a smaller scale. The thought of a dinosaur-sized reptile sleeping on the bed and burping flies had been enough to turn us off.

"It wouldn't be so bad if they were silent," I replied. "But they don't behave like *flies on the wall* should." I hadn't really expected them to listen in silence to secret conversations, record minutiae for subsequent publication in Sunday tabloids, or belly-crawl from A to B for a better camera-angle, but discretion truly is a virtue. "They dive-bomb the cats, get caught in our hair, die noisily spinning on their backs on the window sills and zing off the ceilings. It's exhausting. They're a real *fly in the ointment* of country living."

"I know," Katrina sighed. "I simply can't stand them. I may just acknowledge defeat and spray chemicals over the windows." Much as she enjoyed the country, the attraction of city amenities pulled strongly within her.

"Really!" I said in shock. This was no way for an organic farmer to talk. I resolved to see how our own weapon would perform. Tony derived great satisfaction from his fly swatter that winter. Let me paint the picture.

We are sitting quietly in the living room at the end of the day. I hear one zzzzing by and I catch a sideward glance at Tony. I know he'll do his best to ignore it, in spite of the raised eyebrow. Two, it's harder—it's double the noise. Any more than that, and I know it's game over. A glassy stare comes over him. Fly swatter clenched in his fist, he begins a series of swipes and other acrobatic movements that must give his cardiovascular system a terrific workout. The carcasses get flushed down the toilet (to feed Dragon, the septic tank). A quick glance at the shambles left in the living room tells the most unobservant person that this has been a war zone. Still wielding the fly swatter, he tells me proudly,

"I took no prisoners!"

managing the menagerie

There comes a time in all neighbourly relations when enjoying somebody else's barnyard critters no longer makes up for the rather large droppings on the lawn or the holes they dig. Tony spoke to Matt's father, Brian Farstead, about keeping the animals on their side of the road with a spot of fencing.

"Yes, yes," Brian said calmly. " I understand. We'll get rid of them this weekend. By the way... do you have a shotgun I can borrow?"

The implications were clear! I could not have such shameless murder on my conscience for the sake of wanting my crocuses to bloom. Somewhere between home and Ottawa, I crocodile-tearfully sold Katrina on the benefits of having these animals as pets for Lianne and Sean. I'm not that good an actress, but she was sweetly game.

So, on the coldest day of an already cold spring, Dan, Katrina and the kids came over post-haste for a duck-and-bunny roundup session before their fate was permanently sealed. Dan bagged the ducks—slow and clumsy as they are—without problem.

"Well done!" I said, keen to keep the enthusiasm running high. "I think the bunnies will be a bit harder. I'm not even sure how many we're dealing with. They've done what bunnies do best."

I was right. It was like the parting of the Red Sea. As Lianne and Sean ran around waving their arms in the air, the bunnies fled in all directions. After a monumental effort, we trapped one behind the house. Tony readied a feedbag and string but just as I plopped him in, there was a horrible miscommunication. The bag fell, and the bunny, sensing freedom, bounced out and away in a streak of white fur. I performed an artistic diving tackle, missed completely and uttered a series of expletives worthy of a top-class fishwife. Poor Lianne had never heard such language and stared at me, mouth agape. Bunny stew loomed large on the menu in the Farstead household.

We caught all but one that day in a breathless frenzy of activity. A reliable source of information told me that, on the way home, Dan could be heard muttering under his breath that all he needed was another bunch of non profit-making animals.

The phone rang later that evening. "Uhm," Dan sounded embarrassed. "Don't suppose you've seen your ducks, have you? I just saw them waddle down the drive and turn onto the road. Thought they might be going home."

"Not here," we replied, somewhat concerned.

The following morning, again in the car, Katrina updated me. By now, I was accustomed to the fact that she could talk nineteen to the dozen, put her makeup on and drive significantly above the speed limit at the same time. On the occasional day when she dropped Lianne and Sean off at the sitter's, she added being able to reach round and cuff a miscreant to that list. Her green eyes sparkled with amusement as she told her story. Neighbour Guy Whiteside had called shortly after Dan hung up with us.

"You got some more crazy animals up there?" he asked, remembering the bison episode.

"Huh?" replied Dan, not wanting to divulge how many or which ones.

"Well, I'm wondering if these two ducks are yours," Guy continued. "They arrived this evening, headed for the calf-barn and tucked themselves in for the night."

Katrina giggled, paying only marginal attention to the road ahead. "I bet they're so used to spending the day at your place and crossing the road back to Matt's for the night that they did exactly that. They're already back on our lawn, you know."

The kids play on that lawn. I thought it best to keep quiet.

With the arrival of Canada geese in Guy's fields, the ducks stayed put. The Barbary cob, who hadn't been part of this daily shuttle, found himself alone at the Flansbury farm.

Several weeks later, I caught sight of two Barbary ducks emerging from Dan's pig barn. Was I seeing double?

"He belongs to Arnold Herdman, next door," Katrina sighed. "We've already returned him twice, but he gets back here before we do. Arnold's not thrilled about having his dinner move in with us, but what can we do…?"

And with this musical chairs complete, everybody lived happily ever after.

road to nowhere

Knox Road is a fine example of a rural route. It comes from nowhere and goes nowhere. It meanders through farmlands and bush; it passes century stone homes with beautiful English-style gardens and modern bungalows in freshly minted, treeless settings; it leads to a racehorse stable, a nineteenth century schoolhouse, a meat-cutter's, a strawberry farm and hydroponic tomato farm. All this on the flattest landscape you could ever find. By the time the weary traveller reaches our house, Knox Road is unpaved. Coming from Montreal's devastated roads, we didn't think plain ol', flat ol' gravel would be an issue. However…

Primo, when every other road is clear of snow, Knox still has a thick 'n slick coat of ice. Gravel holds the cool temperature better than asphalt. Tony likes to do handbrake turns on the tight s-bend on the western end and, although we have never actually ended up in the ditch, there are plenty of fingernail-shaped grooves in the dashboard on the passenger side.

Segundo, the snowplow driver clears too wide a shoulder on each side of the road and cuts into our front yard. *He'll* be in the ditch if he's not careful. He's only centimetres from uprooting the telephone pole. And the mailbox has already been sent tumbling into the road. This was on the return pass, so the driver was able to turn a very convenient blind eye. But—and there's always a but—according to Roger, the plow itself is incorrectly adjusted, so wherever there's a bump or hollow in the road, the plow scoops out an equivalent chunk of gravel on its downward bounce, leaving us with a frozen surface looking and feeling like a moonscape. Anything over fifty kilometres an hour—most people go well over ninety—and it'll rattle the teeth right out of your head.

Tertio, in summer, Public Works never puts down sufficient gravel to adequately fill the potholes caused by idiot fast drivers and agricultural equipment. So the washboard effect is here to stay—until the road is paved.

So here I am, cat among the locals, thinking I could get it done in a jiffy and wondering why nobody has tried. I went to my customary source of local *savoir-faire*. Roger's house was moved from the path of Highway 401 construction to its present location on a severed corner of our land and he's lived there since. If anybody knows how to deal with this, I thought, Roger does.

"Better not mention my name," he warned. Apparently, his differences with the Township reached epic proportions decades ago when the Public Works Manager of the day swore that Knox Road would never be paved during his lifetime.

"Whose lifetime?" I asked, wondering if that manager was of Roger's vintage.

Roger shrugged his shoulders, obviously not offended at the implication.

I already knew that Doug Winter was *persona non grata* at council meetings because of the stir he created over something or other. So when Fairlee Road—being half as wide as Knox and a lot less travelled—got a handsome facelift, I began to suspect that these two guys might have sparked some ill-feeling within the bureaucracy.

"Knox is on my wish list," Frank Sorrell, the current Public Works Manager, told me. "Why don't you write to the Council? I can give you some figures on the cost of grading, surface-treatment and asphalting."

Given the reality of the Township's tiny budget, the more affluent tax-base living elsewhere and this ongoing enmity, I wasn't hopeful. Nevertheless, I wrote a knock-your-socks-off letter to Council in time for the next budget meetings that I felt sure would turn the tide in my favour.

"Not addressing the issue of paving Knox is costing the Township and the tax-payer a long-term arm and leg," I told them, in utter diplomatic suicide. Not to mention the cost of the wasted gravel being splashed by the plow onto the lawns, and in our case, nicking the Jetta's expensive new paint job to boot. Of course, I was completely ignored. I'm a woman; I don't work in the area; I don't know the right people; and most of all, I'm not a local. What was I thinking!

I was about to start harassing Frank for the following year's strategy, when he pre-empted me with a phone call.

"Thought you'd want to know," he said. "There's going to be a counter on Knox and a few other roads to measure the traffic."

My heart leapt.

"But," he continued. "I don't know yet when it'll go up. It'll depend on how fast the snow melts."

My heart sank right back down again. The plow would probably knock that box clear into the next township.

I called Roger and the Cantleys, who were also keen to reduce the wear and tear on their shock absorbers.

"Okay, this is the plan. We don't know when, or in fact where, on the road this counter will be, but it's only staying up for twenty-four hours, so everyone keep their eyes peeled. Whoever spots it first calls the others and we all blow a tank of gas rolling backwards and forward over it."

"Agreed," said Steve Cantley. "Hey, if we don't fudge the stats in our favour, people with counters on their roads will and then we won't stand a chance."

March turned into April turned into May. The snow melted into puddles and the counter was nowhere to be seen. I called Frank for a situation update.

"Well," he hesitated. I took a deep breath. I could feel an excuse coming on. "The counter donated to us by Cornwall Township was broken. We thought we could repair it, but it's obsolete and we can't get parts."

I exhaled audibly. Neither of us being blessed with the woes of a video phone, I was grateful that he couldn't see the grimace, too.

"Let's go to Plan B, then," I replied. "Can you root around in your paper trail and find out why Fairlee Road was chosen for surface-treatment?"

"Sure can," he promised.

May turned into June turned into July. I never dared call for the answer. In the meantime, Tony had decided to transfer a pile of rocks from one of our fields over the fence and onto the edge of the ditch under municipal maintenance. Our answering machine filled with irate calls from the Township Office and I thought we'd better lie low for a while.

There's still next year, and the year after that. I can be patient.

twinkle toes

Katrina put her foot to the floor. We were, as usual, well over the speed limit but there were no cops in sight and we were late for class. It's not easy to finish work in Ottawa at five o'clock, pick up Tony and Dan in Ingleside *and* be in Cornwall at six, ready to hit the dance floor.

Dan and Katrina had persuaded us to join them in ballroom dancing lessons, assuming that since we were sporty and hand-to-eye co-ordinated, we should also have rhythm and grace. The Township offered a limited range of adult-oriented municipal activities—euchre (I don't think so!), badminton (been there, done that), and yoga (need more *action*). In view of the meagre choice, dancing sounded like fun.

"The man *always* steps forward with his left foot first," explained Violette, our instructor. She raised a puff of fluorescent pink tulle petticoats, revealing her knees and beyond, and demonstrated the basic Rumba step to Tony.

Tony's attention wavered. He doesn't get much opportunity to see other people's knees these days. Violette whipped round to my side, closely followed by all her petticoats.

"The woman *always* steps back with her right foot first," she continued. Assuming we understood, she tapped out the count to the music with her foot. "Ready... Go!"

Tony, thinking that *always* meant either not him or not in this case, took one monster leap forward with his right foot. He landed firmly on my left foot and I landed on the floor. From my unique vantage point, I wryly observed the other beginners in the class. They might not be glowing advertisements for poise and grace, but the individuals in each couple were both upright, even if their gaze was glued in concentration to their feet. Close enough for a beauty-and-the-beast comparison, Dan and Katrina were putting us to shame with a show of fluid togetherness that only comes with talent or a great deal of practice.

"You know," Violette chided, "you will have to learn the Rumba. Without it, you will never be able to Cha Cha or Mambo."

"Terrific," I thought. "Stymied at Lesson One."

Meanwhile, our friends Tom and Isabelle Maynard of Country Lane Organics, whom Dan and Katrina also introduced to dancing and who were only veterans of one season, whirled away in perfect unison. I liked to think they practised at home until their feet blistered.

"It's because *you* were trying to lead," said Tony, picking me up. "This is one place—possibly the only place—where what I say goes."

I asked Katrina about this during the break.

"Pffff," she said. "I guide Dan all the time, otherwise it gets boring. The trick is to do it subtly enough that he doesn't even realize."

As the weeks progressed, we discovered that the Cha Cha and the Mambo are speeded-up versions of the Rumba; that music doesn't wait for hesitation; and that rhythm and grace are not part of our genetic makeup. We were learning six or seven new steps each week and applying them to round dancing, in which the steps are called. Although this approach did solve the issue of leading, it did nothing for our stress levels as we struggled to remember the name of the step and then execute it in time to the music.

When Violette taught us eight new Jive steps in half an hour, dropped the needle on a record that seemed to play at twice the speed of light and half the class developed two left feet, the need for homework became obvious. This was not the relaxing activity we had anticipated.

"Next week," said Violette, "waltz, foxtrot and tango."

"Yeah," I thought in despair. "For a grand total of about twenty new steps in two hours."

To everybody's amazement, no less our own, our waltz proved to be adequate and our tango even better.

"Hey," said Tony, arching me slightly backwards. "We can actually do this."

"I know," I replied, one arm flung carelessly over his shoulder, head erect, facing away. "Whodathunk?"

I didn't dare breathe in case I broke the spell. Our steps were synchronized, the pace slow and sultry, the body positions suited our natural stiffness and the music spoke of smoky, working-class bars in Buenos Aires and warm Latin nights. Apparently, we were in our element. Satisfaction and pride welled up inside me. At last, we would be able to hold our own in any nightclub in Cornwall.

Do they still play the tango in nightclubs?

playing with fire

"DAN!" cried Katrina, leaning out of the kitchen window. "Come quick. The bus is on fire!"

Dan had a soft spot for that bus. It was a wheelchair-accessible, fully equipped, handicapped-passenger minibus that he had retrofitted to transport and display his vegetables at the Ottawa Organic Farmers' Market. When he and Katrina decided to focus the farm on meat production, it became a beacon of obsolescence.

Tired of watching it die a lingering death on their lawn, Katrina had found an interested buyer—a seniors' residence wanting convert it back to its original use. A representative was on her way over to clinch the deal.

Dan came running from the barn, twisting his ankle on a squeaky toy Sean had left on the lawn. He took one glance at the flames dancing on the hood and yelled "Call 9-1-1" before doing an about-turn to fetch the extinguisher.

What Dan had not told Katrina—nor was he about to—was that instead of letting the engine idle gently to check that it was still in working order, he had placed a brick on the accelerator and walked away. The engine was turning over at an amazing rate of RPMs, giving it more exercise in twenty minutes than it had had all year.

Dan popped his head round the kitchen door, closely followed by the foul smell of burning engine oil.

"It's okay, Pooks," he said, trying hard to sound calm, his face splattered with gobs of fire-retardant foam blown back at him by the wind. "It's under control now. Cancel that 9-1-1 call."

Phone still in hand from her original call, Katrina looked at him doubtfully.

"Are you sure? Don't they need to have actually been here so we can file an insurance claim later?"

She was about to hang up for the second time, picturing fire trucks doing illegal U-turns on Highway 401 somewhere between Morrisburg and Bickham Road, when Dan barrelled back into the kitchen, bucket of water in hand. Katrina had a *déjà-vu* flash of the snowy night he had spent sitting astride their roof, pouring buckets of water down the chimney to douse a fire in the pipe.

"Call 9-1-1," he panted. "It's not under control at all."

"Call 9-1-1 yourself," she retorted, thinking fire fighters had better things to do with their day than make endless U-turns. "What do you think I am? Some kind of idiot?"

By the time the fire trucks roared up the driveway, sirens blaring and lights flashing, any neighbour who was not already at the front gate watching the events unfurl knew that he ought to be. Sean yearned to play with one of those trucks. *He* would really make it do party tricks.

The fire fighters, treating this like a simple practice drill, drenched the bus inside and out, gave Dan a pitying look, shook everybody's hand and were gone again within minutes. The neighbours trudged home, visibly disappointed.

A cursory examination—a more in-depth one was quite superfluous—revealed that the engine compartment and part of the interior were so charred as to be useless, not to mention unsellable.

Katrina could barely contain the annoyance surging within her. Feminine intuition told her that Dan had something to do with this, one way or another. Dan recognized that look and decided there was urgent work to be done in the back field. He knew full well that his only hope of redemption lay in the insurance company. Would it pay up, since the damage was not part of a driving accident, had occurred on their own land and was self-inflicted to boot? If a payment came at all, and if it was close to the selling price, he might not have to spend too many nights on the couch—both literally and figuratively.

A month or so later, the insurance cheque was sitting on the kitchen table when Katrina returned from Ottawa. After dinner, amid a hushed silence, she slowly slit the envelope open. The cheque was only... $800 short of the selling price. She allowed the corners of her mouth to curl up a little, folded the cheque and put it into her purse.

Dan smiled cockily at her, rose from the table and sauntered towards the barn to finish his chores. He had been lucky in more ways than one... this time.

to the rescue

"Hit the brakes!" I cried.

Katrina did exactly that, bringing the car from well over the speed limit to a standstill in record time.

"What? Why?" she cried, checking her dashboard panel for warning indicators.

My seatbelt had functioned to perfection and had pinned me to the seat in a stranglehold.

"There's a turtle on the roadside back there" I said lamely. "It'll get run over. We have to save it."

Inexplicably, Katrina's seatbelt had *not* plastered her to her seat. She swivelled round to get a better look at the mound in the long stretch of flat, straight road leading from the city. If it weren't for the trees in the way, I swear it would be possible to see Ottawa from Ingleside.

"Goodness!" she said. "I've never seen one that big. Let me back up."

The reverse gear on Katrina's Taurus is equal to her fifth forward gear. We went from point A to point B at warp speed. The brakes proved themselves up to the task once again as the car teeter-tottered on the shocks. Those tires would never be perfectly round again. Mind you, this car has seen a blur of potholes and railway tracks so it's likely their roundness was only ever a brief illusion.

The turtle was indeed a big 'un. Not that I had any desire to put it there, but I doubted it would fit into a standard oven—and that's not counting the head and tail that were neatly tucked inside the carapace. I didn't see any way of moving it to safety without picking it up.

"Careful," cried Katrina, sticking her head out of the car window. "Those things aren't called snapping turtles for nothing. I'm staying right here!" She wound the window up again and settled in for the show.

I approached the turtle from behind—wanting the element of surprise on my side. In a lightning move I never expected from such a lumbering beast, it whipped round to face me, reared up and snapped its beak mere centimetres from my face. The element of surprise was indeed on my side—but not the way I expected.

I stepped back—mostly to collect my scattered thoughts. The turtle stepped forward, beak open, eyes black. The audience behind me filled me with false courage. I stepped forward. The turtle stepped back. I had never danced with a turtle before but the two of us certainly had better rhythm than Tony and I did. This was the closest I'd ever been to a Rumba.

Katrina wound the window down again and opened her mouth to speak.

"No," I said, silencing her. "I have a cunning plan. Watch this."

I retrieved my sports kit from the car and pulled out a sweaty t-shirt that I passed over the turtle's back and over its head. The beak snapped shut on it. I'd never had a tug-of-war with a turtle either. I dragged it a few steps before it released the t-shirt—complete with turtle slobber and gaping hole. That beak must be very sharp as well as snappy. I repeated the procedure.

Katrina stuck her head out of the window again.

"You're going in the wrong direction," she said. "You're taking it back to where it came from."

I couldn't believe my ears.

"Are you kidding me?" I snorted. "You think it cares? You think *I* care? I just want it off the road so it doesn't become a pancake!"

Already, the turtle was losing patience with this game. I spun it around and tugged it back across the road and down the shoulder where it glared furiously at me. Had it been able to spit like a camel, I'm sure it would have unleashed a shower of saliva that would have slimed me from top to bottom. Instead, I took my cue and legged it back to the car before it decided to follow me and wreak another kind of revenge.

"There!" I said to Katrina, slamming the door behind me. "Happy?"

My t-shirt was in shreds and I nearly had my nose bitten off by a reptile. She, on the other hand, had watched the whole show from front-row seating. No wonder she could barely catch her breath from laughing.

"Very," she giggled, pleased as punch with her little joke.

As the car squealed away at a speed that would make Michael Schumacher proud, I checked in the rear-view mirror to see the falling sun glint on a shiny turtle shell that was heading right back onto the road again. This was not a turtle that wanted to be saved.

the puttin'-down-roots years

a garage, a garage, my kingdom for a garage

"This would be a logical place to build the garage," said Tony. "But we'd have to cut down that little thicket of Manitoba maples."

The logical place we had found was on the east side of the house, fairly close to the road. It was the one small area of our lot *not* encumbered by trees (Manitoba maples or other), fences, hydro poles, roadside mailboxes and other paraphernalia. And it was right on our gravelled driveway. Not only was it a logical place, it was the *only* place. The other sites we crossed off the list were behind the house on the east side—but the car would have to pass over the water-line from the well to the house each time and we didn't like that idea; and the west side—through the cherry grove and the leach field for the septic system. Tony certainly wasn't about to sacrifice his precious cherries and, again, the car shouldn't to-and-fro over the leach field.

"Manitoba maples are weeds," I replied ruthlessly. "To hell with 'em!" Those blasted seedlings grow aggressively everywhere. If I didn't hunt them down and yank them out every couple of weeks, their long taproot made them tough to pull once they were established. And once they were established, no amount of cutting, snapping or otherwise damaging them could cause their ultimate demise. Hence that little thicket.

Armed with a bunch of measurements, Tony called the Township office to find out about the building code requirements on exactly how far back from the road a garage has to be.

"Fifteen metres back from the roadway," replied the clerk.

"Really!" replied Tony. "Well, that kind of makes a snowblower a necessity around here, doesn't it?" The idea of shovelling fifteen metres of snow several times a winter wasn't at the top of his list of fun things to do. "Hmm," he continued, looking out of the kitchen window at the proposed site and my pretty little flowerbed of bleeding hearts and irises. "In that case, the well-head would be in the exact centre of the garage. That'll never do."

"You might be able to go ahead if you get a variance," suggested the clerk.

"Sounds good," replied Tony, much cheered. "What's that?"

"You pay two hundred and fifty dollars. We convene a meeting of councillors to issue a temporary construction permit. Then we send letters to all owners of properties within seventy-five metres of the proposed construction, seeking their approval."

"Oh," said Tony, now much deflated. "Expensive rubber stamp."

"So," the clerk continued, ignoring the remark. "If nobody opposes the building, you can go ahead. If you try to construct without proper authorization, the Township can take you to court. If you want to sell the property later on and the buyer's lawyer sends a letter to the Township asking about the legality of the buildings, you could lose the sale while everything gets sorted out!"

Tony was beginning to feel cornered. He doesn't do well when he's cornered. Tension pulsed down the phone line. He glared at the receiver and tightened his grip.

"Your options are: submit two hundred and fifty bucks, build farther back or don't build at all," she finished.

Click.

Furious, Tony went to see Roger. His garage is built so close to the road there's barely room between the two for a car. How did he get away with it? As with everything in the country, we were finding out, there was a story here. Roger admitted to having had "words" with the Public Works Manager of the time, several decades back.

"Oh yes," he said. "Can you believe it? They were ready to have me pay the two hundred and fifty bucks when a friend told me that there was already a garage on that very spot. So the new one is exempt under the grandfather rule." He continued, muttering under this breath, "Only it beats me why nobody at the Township office mentioned it to me at the time…"

We filed that thought under "Township Fundraising" and will, of course, contribute to that account when the time comes.

the early bird never gets enough sleep

It's not that we're lazy, but our internal clocks don't ring automatically at five o'clock in the morning and throw us out of bed bright-eyed, bushy-tailed and ready to split logs ten minutes later. It must be a genetic or environmental mutation. Tony and I don't have the genes and we haven't been in the environment anywhere near long enough. All our neighbours get up with the birds—if not before.

Try as he might, Tony had been unable to crack the concrete slab and retaining concrete blocks of the front deck with a sledgehammer. It sloped farther away from the house with each passing year. Soon, it might take part of the house with it as it separated, iceberg-like, from the main structure.

"D'you think Guy would take a look," Tony asked Dan. Dan occasionally worked for his neighbour Guy Whiteside's construction company when farm chores were low on the list of priorities and the need for fast cash was conversely high.

"I'll see if he'll bring his backhoe over," replied Dan, wondering why Tony didn't call him directly. He hadn't yet experienced one of Tony's *fortés*—creating loops of information.

On an autumn evening long after Tony had forgotten this request, Dan phoned (on Katrina's wise advice) to warn us that he and Guy would be in our yard at seven the next morning.

"Seven!!!" thought Tony. "On a Sunday! Don't these people sleep?"

From tried-and-tested experience, Katrina was wary of the trouble these two men (three, assuming Tony heard the alarm clock) could get up to with such a large toy. Guy must be an insomniac. The backhoe was sitting on our lawn at six-thirty and we were bounced out of bed by a tremendous THUNGG-UNG-UNG-G-G. The comparatively pathetic ring of the alarm clock was forgotten in the *mêlée*. Under other circumstances, I might have suspected an earthquake.

Tony and I threw on our dressing gowns and tumbled outside to offer moral support. Guy and Dan were sporting grins wide enough to hook over their ears. Busily handling all those levers simultaneously, Guy—small, wiry frame, toque, grizzled beard and blue, blue eyes—looked like an elf at Santa's conveyor belt.

We watched, through bleary eyes, as the two guys and their hardware turned our already not terribly level lawn into a battlefield. Now that the concrete blocks were split apart, a veritable flood of rubble flowed out from behind the cracks. Try as he might, Guy was unable to pick any of it up without taking away large chunks of sod as well. To add a flair for the dramatic to the situation, the blocks had been bonded to the foundation of the house. The more (and the deeper) Guy scooped, the more of the stone foundation fell away.

"Rubble, rubble, toil and trouble." My mind subconsciously modernized Shakespeare's *Macbeth*. How prophetic. Our eyes were open now.

"Okay, Guy," yelled Tony above the crunch of metal scoop on stone. "We'll leave it right there."

Guy jumped out and posed dramatically in front of his machine, legs apart, hands on hips, waiting for approval. His supervisory job done, Dan joined him in a similar stance. Neither man had stopped smiling since they arrived.

We surveyed the damage. The lawn, where it wasn't cratered with scoop-holes, was strewn with rocks and rubble. Instead of a deck, we now had a below-grade cavity, an awning held up with two studs and a foundation sufficiently breached to allow access to the basement for over-wintering mice.

Dan and Guy waved cheerily as they drove away. It was seven-thirty. They had done half a day's work already. Tony and I went back to bed.

gun wars

The man on the doorstep looked half-wild, half naked and babbled like an idiot. It was an uncommon way to begin an acquaintance. Tony had seen him stagger out of our woods on this miserable autumn evening and beaten him to the porch door.

"Are you okay?" he asked.

The man was in his early thirties, exhausted and quite incoherent. Every pore of his body dripped from the diluvial rain. This was definitely the wrong side of eccentric.

"Whatever had happened," Tony thought, "the explanation should be well worth hearing."

The man's remaining strength ebbed like molasses out of a jar. Tony reached forward and grabbed him just before his knees thunked on the concrete steps. The explanation would have to wait. Rehydrating him was more urgent.

"What the hell happened to you?" Tony tried again, now that the man was able to pry his tongue from the roof of his mouth. It felt somehow ironic that a person could be so dehydrated during such a downpour.

"Where am I?

"Knox Road."

"Don't know it."

"How did you get here?"

"Walked."

The tin roof on the porch amplified the noise of the torrential downpour, making conversation difficult. Tony waited in hot anticipation for the rest of the story. None came.

"With only one shoe?" prodded Tony, nodding at the man's sodden sock. "And from where?"

"Oh, that…" began the man. "I was hunting on my uncle's land this morning…"

"A-ha!" thought Tony. "There's more to this than meets the eye."

"…And I got lost. And my boot got sucked off in the mud. And I've got a ton of blisters. And cuts. And splinters too, probably." A drop of water ran down his forehead to the tip of his nose and hung there for a moment before he blew it off.

He glanced in my direction—I was wearing my best disapproving look—and then back at Tony.

"Could I get a lift home, pleeeeze?"

Tony poured him into the car.

"Pssst," I whispered after him. "Make sure you find out the rest."

I was keen to hear the story in spite of my objections to his activities. We don't allow any kind of hunting on our land. I don't understand the thrill-of-the-kill, or the provider instinct. As a species, I'd like to think we've evolved beyond that. Nor do I understand the sport in using laser-sights, power-rifles, night-vision goggles, pheromones and blinding lights to gain the advantage over an animal who, all things being equal, has a way better chance of surviving alone in the bush than the raggedy specimen who landed at our door. On the other hand, if half the neighbourhood hunters are twice as efficient as this fellow, then the local fauna is pretty safe.

In the privacy of the car, windshield wipers banging away at full tilt, the male bonding began. Obviously, the man hadn't wanted to tell his story in front of me. I didn't think my disapproval radiated that far.

"How can it be fun to hunt in the pouring rain?" asked Tony, himself now soaked from his short walk to the car.

"Well…" he replied, somewhat cockily, considering he was leaching water all over the car seat. "It doesn't normally bother me. But this time I got lost back there. I started sweating in my waterproof suit and it turned into a steam bath. I couldn't stand it any more. I was wetter in it than out, so I took it off bit by bit as I went."

Tony tactlessly remarked on the foolhardiness of this move.

"Yeah, well, sometimes you don't think straight," came the offended reply. "I took my t-shirt off too. It got cold, wet and useless right away."

He didn't notice Tony roll his eyeballs.

"But," he added, "I think I hit a deer somewhere back there."

The car hydroplaned as Tony nearly drove off the road in horror.

"On *our* land?"

"Dunno. I didn't see it go down and I couldn't keep up with it. I'll come back tomorrow and see if I can find it. I have to come back anyway to look for my crossbow."

In the fracas, nobody had noticed that this was one hunter without a weapon.

"I wouldn't bother," replied Tony dryly. "You'll never find either. And the forecast is for more rain."

As he left the soggy man in the care of his relatives, he made a mental note that we really should take the time to mark our boundaries. Who knows how many other loaded weapons live in our woods.

here a turkey, there a turkey

'Twas the week before Thanksgiving, and all over the land… turkeys were being trucked to their final destination.

'Twas now the week *after* Thanksgiving, and in this particular corner of the land, Tony and I were preparing a belated celebration for his carnivorous sisters. I had been unable to persuade them into a vegetarian feast and reluctantly agreed to roast a you-know-what. From the kitchen window, as we peeled potatoes and carrots in feverish haste, we could see a living, breathing you-know-what quietly enjoying the fresh air and sunshine at the roadside.

A car came to a screeching halt in our driveway. Tony's sister, Susie, burst through the front door.

"Guys, guys!" she could hardly get the words out. "There's this humungous turkey—sitting there like a rock—just up the road."

"Yeah, Susie," we replied, without looking up from the mountain of peelings. "There are lots of wild turkeys around here. She's probably back in the woods by now."

This was not a satisfactory answer. "Yeah, but… it's right *there*… NOW!" Susie insisted forgetting that, even if we started right away—not to mention doing the deed, plucking and gutting—the number of minutes per pound it takes to cook a turkey would delay dinner somewhere into the following week.

"Susie!" We looked at her sternly.

Blessed with the same stubborn streak as Tony, Susie coaxed me up the road on the pretext of going for a walk. We didn't have far to go. The turkey was now sitting on Roger's lawn gazing into his basement window.

"This really is a very fine bird," I thought.

"What are we going to do with her?" asked Susie. I have long held the theory that most city-dwelling meat-eaters would suddenly explore vegetarianism if faced with actually killing an animal. Susie's retreat from bloodthirsty aggression was a round-one victory. My animal-rescue instincts flared up.

"We are going to take her home," I replied firmly, knowing full well that hunters were one of the exceptions to my theory, that we were in the middle of game season and that she wouldn't last long on the road. No trigger-happy hunter would drive by, slam on the brakes and blast away at her. Not on my watch.

Roger's wife, Mary, saw that this might have some entertainment value and sat herself down on the porch, knitting in hand, to observe the proceedings. To her great disappointment, we gently—and surprisingly easily—shooed the turkey down towards our land, into the chicken pen and closed the door.

"Ha!" we thought, puffed with success.

Tony looked at me reproachfully. "What are we going to do with a turkey who is going to eat us out of house and chicken feed?"

"I don't know, sweetie," I replied. "But she'll be happy and safe here."

I was disappointed to find her beating a path back and forth at the edge of the run, and the chickens cross-eyed with displeasure. A brief family meeting followed at which it was decided not to pen a bird who had known freedom, and that she should have her chance at a real life. I opened the pen door and she ambled out. She strolled towards Matt's barn and back towards Roger's place where she plopped herself down in front of his basement window again.

Then, and only then, did it occur to me to check if she were really a wild turkey or domestic. "She's a domestic bird!" I cried, reference book in hand. "She must have fallen off the back of a turkey truck. She'll never make it in the wild, she doesn't have the smarts. We have to get her back!"

Tony and Susie stared at me incredulously, although Susie did pronounce herself game for a second attempt. Well, once caught, twice shy. The wretched bird was having none of it. Susie and I chased her from Roger's lawn into Steve Cantley's garage, round and round his lilacs, over to the Winters' and back to Roger's. He and Mary were having lunch by then. But this was better than any reality TV. As we cornered her on his deck, all sorts of advice came floating through the window from the faces pressed against the glass. That fairground game came to mind—the one where you hit a spot with a mallet as hard as possible that flings a marker up a pole to record the force of the blow. As quickly as I pounced, she leapt straight up out of my grasp like a rubber ball. The advice from the window began to contain suppressed giggles. We were beaten. She would have to fend for herself.

Later, as Susie and I were planting the lilacs that were eventually to become the windbreak on the west side, I heard Tony call from the deck. "Uhm, Sylviane. You have to come and see this."

Steve was walking briskly down the road, the turkey tucked neatly under one arm—and sitting quietly, no less.

"Cornered her in the garage," he said smoothly. "No trouble at all." As if he caught turkeys every day for a living, which I know for sure he doesn't.

So back she went into the coop. Dusk was falling and the chickens were already asleep. "Perfect," I thought. "She can at least stay there until morning without causing mayhem. We'll call Dan later to find out what turkeys eat."

The very instant I slammed the door shut on her for the second time, Steve clapped his hand to his forehead. "Oh no," he said. "I know where I've seen that turkey before. She belongs to the Buchanans, next door to us."

Great, Steve. You couldn't have thought of that *before* releasing her in the coop! I was giddy at the thought of having to catch her yet again.

Carol Buchanan, however, was delighted that not only had there been a sighting, but that she was in (relative) captivity. "I'll send Jasper along to pick her up. We're going to have her for Christmas," she confided conspiratorially over the phone.

Jasper was already eighty-three when he made the local news by accidentally spending the night in his woods a couple of Novembers ago. He had wanted to check his land for loggers and got turned around. Only the box of matches in his shirt pocket had made the experience less excruciating than it might otherwise have been.

Jasper pulled up on our doorstep in a gleaming white Caddy and without his sorely needed hearing-aid.

Tony filled his lungs. "D'YA THINK YOU CAN HELP ME CATCH HER?"

"EH?" came the reply.

Further conversation was pointless.

Only a cartoon can adequately portray the following scene. Tornados of dust, enough flying feathers for a pillow fight, panicked, screaming chickens under the firm belief their end had come, and people plunging into the eye of the storm.

Tony straightened up and squared his jaw. This was going nowhere and Jasper was too old and stiff to play this game. He lunged, grabbed the turkey by the tail and screwed her into the ground with his other hand. In that lightening-quick manoeuvre, the turkey lost its dignity and tail feathers, and Tony gained a handsome fistful to add to his proverbial cap.

As the Caddy inched slowly home with Tony and the bird in the passenger seat, I couldn't help thinking, "Bet this is the first live turkey on record to ride in a Caddy!"

'Twas the week before Christmas, and all over the land…

gone with the wind (or wuthering heights)

After Guy and Dan removed the deck, Tony jammed a stud under the outer corners of the ugly awning to prevent it from collapsing in front of the door like wilted lettuce.

"What are you going to do about the up-force from the wind, sweetie?" I asked, thinking that, without a collection of rocks weighing it down in strategic places, the lightest breeze would take it up like Mary Poppins and her umbrella.

"Nothing," replied Tony. "The wind doesn't blow that way, so why bother!"

"All righty then." I couldn't be bothered to argue this one. We were going to replace the awning anyway. If it blew off, so be it.

It was eerily warm for a December day. At twenty degrees on the plus side, it was worth being outside, on our bikes, wearing shorts, mowing the lawn, having a picnic, anything! Now I know what a Chinook feels like. My knotted muscles relaxed in the warmth of the sun. My neck reappeared from inside my shoulders. It was short-lived. Those same poor muscles tightened up again the very next

day in a brain-busting minus eighteen degrees, not counting
the wind-chill.

The wind increased during the day in reverse
proportion to the fall in temperature, that is, pretty darn fast.
The awning heaved up and down in perfect chronometric
time with the gusts. Like a lung. I winced. Tony ignored
both the awning and me. Nobody likes to be so wrong. As
the evening progressed, the awning breathed more and
more deeply; it groaned and creaked under the strain—a
lung with acute bronchitis. Thunk! Thunk! The studs fell
away. It was on its own now.

"D'you think I should check it out?" I asked Tony, in a
moment of insanity.

Tony didn't even look up from his plumbing efforts in
the laundry room—possibly because he had driven a
drywall screw into the hot water pipe for the shower and
had a small flood on his hands.

"And do what?" There was a certain irritating logic to
that question/answer. The wind was indeed frightening. I
would be the one sucked up like Mary Poppins, only not
half as dignified.

I didn't sleep a wink. The wind whistling past (and
through) the house forced against the bedroom windows. It
was unnerving—as was the constant screech of awning
materials grinding against each other. The house flexed as
the gusts pushed harder. I curled into the fetal position
under the duvet wondering if, in case anything happened to
the house, we should be hiding in the bathtub as we had
been advised by people who have read books about, but
never actually experienced, a hurricane. My mind wanders
to strange places when I can't sleep. This time it went to

Kansas—to *The Wizard of Oz*. I doubted if Dorothy and Toto had hidden in the bathtub, or if they even had one. I compared our house to the Kansas farmhouse. The resemblance was uncanny. OMIGOD, like it or not, we were going to Oz!

Then… an ear-splitting crunch. Simultaneously the bed was shunted sideways and the house wrenched in the same direction. My eyes snapped open. It was four-fifteen. Had we landed in Oz? What was the alternative? Tony snored stertorously. Finally able to relax, I followed suit.

The following morning, a Sunday, Matt's brother, Rick, beat on the kitchen door at eight-thirty. Will nobody let us sleep! He pointed out the damage to us piece by piece. Kansas may have looked somewhat like this after the farmhouse was lifted. The remains of awning were plastered against Roger's fence—easily fifty metres away. On its way, it had rolled over the Jetta causing significant bodywork damage, snapped the washing lines, collapsed the fencing on the vegetable garden and strewn body parts all over the field. While we were impressed with the toll this would take on our wallets, the nature of the actual urgency escaped us so we returned to bed as though nothing had happened.

We would call the insurance company at a more respectable hour.

the visitor

"Oh, what now!" railed Tony irritably, followed by a salvo of unprintable expletives. The sump pump in the basement had been running for nearly twenty minutes—abnormal even for the inflow of spring meltwater. I sighed and followed him down the basement steps.

Groping through the murky darkness, dying flashlight between his teeth, he lowered his hand into the cold, inky water of the pump pit—and jumped back with a cry, almost knocking himself out on a mighty beam. The hairs on the back of his neck bristled to attention like iron filings to a magnet. Something… something soft had touched his hand.

I had already climbed back up the steps two by two in my haste to escape the unknown. As a European, I'm a firm believer in ghosts and things that go bump in the night. How can a house this old not have stories to tell? Fact: the Flansbury home has babies, presumably—hopefully!— stillbirths, buried under the front lawn. And we haven't finished renovating, so there are bound to be secrets yet to uncover. My fertile imagination doesn't have far to stretch to believe that tangible energies live here with us. Tony denies having any such frailties.

The sump pump quivered noisily, distracting him. Nonetheless, he took a long, deep breath and steeled himself before inching forward gingerly, cautiously, for a peek into the darkness.

The flickering light shone into a pair of blinking eyes. A wee mouse had dislodged the float when it fell into the pit. Tony exhaled audibly. So much for no frailties!

I suppose other country folk would have just left the wee mousey there to meet his (un)natural end and possibly become an unquiet spirit himself. Instead, somewhat pale and shaky though he still felt, Tony fished the mouse out with a strainer, proving just how versatile kitchen utensils can be, flipped him into a plastic bag and released him in the woodshed.

It's even money as to who, of the three of us, had the bigger fright.

a roof over our heads

The day the summer's brutal drought ended and the heavens unleashed two months worth of frustration was the day Guy Whiteside showed up to replace our rusty metal roof. Contractors don't have finely-tuned control over their availability and had Guy not been considered one-of-us through his association with Dan, we might have felt somewhat put upon. For Tony, Dan's reputation had been sealed in the early days when, on one of their outings, Dan had rooted around his truck and come up with a head of garlic in guise of a snack. Dumbfound, Tony watched him eat it, clove by clove, and enjoy it as though it were gumdrops. Guy's reputation rested inauspiciously on the deck incident. Elsewhere in the neighbourhood, however, his word was bond, so we chose to go with the majority.

"How reliable are your tarps," asked Tony, not wanting to wake up in a soggy bed.

Guy raised one eyebrow. Message understood. He was sent away with a small insect in his ear. He reappeared in time for the first deep frost. Was he doing this on purpose? Tony sighed. It was mid-October, getting colder by the day and my parents, due to arrive from the UK in three weeks, would not take kindly to sleeping under the stars.

In order to position the four new skylights that would be part of this funky green tin roof, the upstairs ceilings had to come down to expose the beams. Now we knew there was Zonalite insulation in them thar ceilings; the granola-like particles would settle noisily every now and then. Stark memories of the living room reno returned. For reasons we already know, this would not be a pleasant task.

Our anticipation of a quick and easy job was once again foiled.

"We know one thing for sure," said Tony, from the top of his ladder. "Whoever renovated—and I use the term loosely—the upstairs had no concept of cause-and-effect."

"Meaning...?" I asked.

"Meaning that they put the ceilings up everywhere before they put the dividing walls up. Meaning that we have to tear down the walls to even get access to the whole ceiling. Meaning that this is going to be a helluva job."

Tony was getting understandably frustrated and we hadn't started yet. In a cathartic move, he plunged the crowbar into the decrepit aspenite boards and ripped them to shreds.

"Oh, and by the way, those very same walls were built on top of the carpet," he finished.

What had started out as a new roof, to be done by a contractor, was now ballooning into a renovation of the entire upstairs, by us. As Tony's head poked through the ceiling and into the attic, a muffled voice wafted back down. It wasn't a happy-sounding voice.

"Well, I now know where all those cluster flies come from. There are hundreds of thousands of them up here. They must settle in for the winter."

In the meantime, however, once woken from their hibernation, those same hundreds of thousands turned into swarms that attached themselves to every available source of light. The bedroom windows blacked out and day turned into night. Tony's vocabulary turned all colours of the rainbow as he filled the shop-vac twice.

"I'll be doing something about that—like plugging every little tiny crack to the outdoors. That should get rid of 'em."

Guy had promised the job would be done in two days. When I returned from Ottawa after Day One, a very small fraction of the roof was green. The guys were huddled around the only installed skylight like boy scouts around a campfire. On the ground, Guy's jaw was set. His blue eyes were as cold as the weather. I believe he was rather regretting his glib forecast. Putting skylights in a tin roof is not run-of-the-mill and the learning curve on that first one was close to vertical.

The sun went down. The tarps went up. The guys left. As the day's gentle breeze hardened into a cold October wind, the tarps danced over the new plywood and countless draughts laughed in our faces. The upstairs was now one great big empty loft-like space with very little to separate us from the great outdoors. We could see our breath in bed.

Guy was almost as good as his word. He whipped the guys into shape and finished in two-and-a-half days. In that time, the house was transformed from an ugly duckling into a swan. The green tin shone like a beacon under the autumn sun and light poured into the loft area. It was brilliant.

It was also unliveable. As nighttime lows fell to minus ten degrees Celsius or thereabouts, heating proved futile.

Daylight shone in through the vented ridge cap. We started camping on an inflatable mattress in the living room, close to the wood-stove.

By the time my parents arrived, approximately half the insulation was fitted. There was nowhere for them to sleep that provided both humane conditions and privacy. I made up our upstairs bed with polar fleece sheets, a duvet and two blankets. They would be toasty as long as no appendages escaped the confines of the bed. In fact, the temperature rose to more seasonal numbers during their visit for which my father, whose Mauritian background had not prepared him for the Canadian climate, was deeply thankful.

Tony and I camped downstairs for over a month while he rebuilt the attic floor and finished the insulation. The roof saga was over. The remodelling of the upstairs was about to begin. But that's another story.

if it sounds too good to be true, it probably is

THUMP! THUMP! THUMP! on our front door. At eight o'clock on Boxing Day morning, after returning from a bellyful Christmas celebration in Montreal only a few hours before, we weren't terribly interested in finding out who it might be.

THUMP! THUMP! Why is it people never use the beautiful, not to mention expensive, brass bell hanging by the porch door instead of barrelling blindly past it to beat on the kitchen door instead? Maybe it was urgent…

The one eye I unwillingly pried open revealed this enormous fellow. Short, but unbelievably stocky—whose thick, meaty hands could easily strangle a tree trunk and toss it carelessly over his shoulder when he was done. His toque stretched thinly over his head down to his eyelids. I wasn't awake enough to look, but assumed he had plumber's cleavage too. He mumbled something about concrete.

"No thanks," I mumbled feebly back, somewhat cowed and treating this like one of those awful solicitation phone calls. "I'm sure we already have some." He wasn't big enough to act as a draught-stopper. The cold December air swept through the kitchen and up my nightclothes. All I wanted to do was close the door and go back to bed.

Instead of leaving, he pointed in the direction of the hole in our foundation left by Dan and Guy—another source of cold December air. Foraging rodents had left tiny pathways in the dusting of snow from the bird feeder to the hole, or in other words, from the restaurant to the hotel. "Me an' me boys, we can push some concrete into that 'ole fer three hunnert bucks an' fix up the rest of yer cracks," he repeated.

I smelled a bargain. This is not necessarily a good thing. I'm a notoriously poor judge of character and have been done over more times than I care to remember. The other eye snapped open.

"I got teams working on two 'ouses up the road an' we got concrete left over."

This sounded far too good to be true. That it was barely dawn on a legal holiday didn't ring nearly enough alarm bells. I told him to come back in an hour, flipped Tony out of bed and we both went to see Steve Cantley who was having his chimney pointed.

Steve was less than impressed. A habitually early riser himself, he had been caught horizontally digesting his last meal when this fellow called. Sadly realizing that constant supervision was key to getting the job done, he had grabbed a very un-Boxing Day-like breakfast that he was now consuming in his truck—the only source of both warmth and a clear-line-of-sight outside the house.

"They have no tools," he said, his voice reaching an incredulous tremolo. "I even had to loan them a bucket! And if I turn my back for a minute, they're sat down smoking."

The allure of not having the wind whistle through the basement in the middle of winter almost offset this far-from-glowing recommendation. We pondered the possibility of concrete setting properly in sub-zero temperatures, among the other difficulties presented by doing this sort of job in less than ideal climatic conditions. I pictured concrete oozing gently from the foundation to lie on the lawn like a lava flow—no source of beautification for our already grim-looking front yard. We resolved to ask some right pertinent questions on this fellow's return.

As Tony tapped round the house with a hammer explaining the scope of the job, closely followed by the behemoth, it became clear from his answers that concrete was not this man's main line of work. In retrospect, his crew were probably snow removers forced by the lack of white stuff that winter to put food on the table any which way they could. Nonetheless…

"Twelve hunnert bucks," said the giant firmly. This was a long, long way from his original price, especially from one so obviously inexperienced in the trade he was proposing to ply. Tony blinked. Apparently, inflation was running high that day.

"I think not. Guy Whiteside will do it for nine hundred," he retorted, pulling a random figure out of his head and hoping that, if asked, Guy would do it for a whole lot less in compensation for the mental torture of having to look day in and day out at the mess he had left behind.

"Pah!" came the reply, arm flung dismissively as he headed back to his truck. He spun around. "All right then. Seven hunnert. Last offer."

Tony looked at him and drove the final nail in the coffin. "Of course, you'll provide a written guarantee of the work."

When the carbon monoxide from the truck spinning its wheels in the driveway and leaving two deep furrows in the slush had finished making us cough, we congratulated each other on a job well (that is, not) done.

cold heart(h)ed robbery

"This is the last of the firewood," said Tony one brisk March evening, bringing in a few meagre sticks.

Thanks to the uninsulated roof leaking untold BTUs well into December, we had made a serious dent in our woodpile too early in the season. Far from being the *El-Niño* winter the so-called experts predicted, winter was proving long and bitter. Even though the sun gained strength daily, temperatures were still in the minus-teens at night.

"Paul," I pleaded with our wood supplier. "What can you give us that's dry and will actually burn, not sizzle?"

"Nothing," he replied cruelly. "I don't have a stick left for sale."

"But we don't have enough to see us through." I hoped to tug a little on his heartstrings, and if that failed, use feminine wiles to get the job done.

"You and everybody else," he replied, oblivious. "I've seen people with wheelbarrows by the side of the road collecting blow-downs. You can't use that stuff. It's soggy—a waste of time. Anyway, I can give you this guy's phone number. He might have some left."

He did. We bought. We wasted our money. The tiny logs sizzled and frothed madly in the stove. By the time a lonely flame flickered some warmth in our direction, it was time for bed.

"I have an idea," said Tony, cocooned in the depths of the sofa one evening. He had been spending enough time with Dan recently for the two men to feed bad ideas off each other. I didn't expect anything good to come of this.

"Parks Ontario will be tapping the sugar bush at the bird sanctuary this spring, right?"

"Right."

We knew this because the blow-downs from the Ice Storm had been neatly chopped and piled next to the old sugar shack, and the old wide-board buildings recently brought into working order. Set five hundred metres back from the road, nestled in the maple forest atop a small knoll—the very same knoll at the bottom of which the ski trail took a sharp right-hand turn that I could never negotiate vertically—and equipped with a horse barn and hand-pump well, Tony and I had explored these buildings and regretted their lack of use. Now, they were ready to come to life again and provide warmth and fun for the locals. Anyway, I estimated there were about seventy cords of wood waiting to turn maple sap into maple syrup.

"I see where you're going with this," I continued. "But you're not considering a couple of major obstacles. One, it's not our wood. Two, how do you plan to get it out of there?"

"I've thought of that," Tony replied. "We can do the wheelbarrow-thing too. We can tie it to the roof of the car after filling the trunk with wood." I noted that he hadn't actually thought about my first point but I was too chilled to care and the weather forecast included yet another cold snap.

The wheelbarrow-thing was a bust. It wouldn't stay on the roof of the car without sliding down the windshield, and we thought it would be inappropriate to drive like that. Instead, if we each carried one handle of our big wood tote, we could potentially haul seven to nine logs at a time. So off we went into the sanctuary woods, nonchalantly swinging our tote.

"So what do we do if somebody sees us?" I asked Tony. "I mean, it's pretty obvious…"

"Toss the tote and pretend it's not ours."

Well, only five of those mammoth logs fit into the tote, each one weighing the equivalent of twenty bricks. Considering those trees had been dead for several years, they still contained a surprising amount of moisture. There was no way I would be tossing anything as I struggled to keep up my end of the deal. During one of the many pauses I needed to walk the five hundred metres back to the car, I heard a vehicle pull into the parking lot. The door slammed shut. Tony and I prepared to drop our booty and run. A chainsaw started up. So… we weren't the only ones borrowing wood from the government. Our method, however, sounded far less labour-intensive.

I loaded those five wretched logs into the trunk while Tony checked out the competition.

"Someone's cutting down a tree just on the other side of the parking area," he said, back at the car. "He's certainly got his work cut out for him. There's no way that wood will be dry enough to use."

As coincidence would have it, the Parks security patrol vehicle turned into the parking lot at that very instant and two beefy guys tumbled out. I lowered the lid of the trunk to hide our ill-gotten gains and innocently dusted off the tote. Tony shoved me into the passenger seat, nodded a greeting at the guys and sped away without a backward glance.

Did we get our just deserts for our illicit heat source, for abandoning a fellow wood-poacher to his fate? Yes. The government's wood sucks, too. We shivered until May.

enough is enough

By the time summer came round again, Tony and I had had enough of Matt's animals. To recap:

Katy, the German Shepherd, lived alone in the barn for an entire summer and barked twenty-four hours a day. Kurt and Cameron, the cats who were supposed to keep the barn mouse-free, saw the good living across the road and moved in with us. The Dachshund stayed in the barn for afternoons on end, yip-yipping rhythmically and drove us mental. The horses broke their fencing with monotonous regularity to gallop across our lawn and vegetable garden. The ducks and bunnies have been documented elsewhere. At least, we thought that problem was licked until seven roosters and an equal number of hens appeared in spring. The roosters gathered underneath our bedroom window a touch before the crack of dawn and serenaded us at the top of their lungs. The hens ravaged the garden. We spent our days chasing them out.

I lamented to Katrina and George Wilson, my new carpooling buddy.

"Let me tell you a hypothetical story," grunted George. "Once upon a time, I kept finding my neighbour's cows in my pasture. I called him to come and get them, as any neighbour would do. He knew I'd call so he never did anything about his fences. The next time his cows got loose, I drove them way into the bush. Took him a week to find them, but the fences were mended right away."

He looked at me meaningfully. Another one who only spends a fraction of his driving time actually looking at the road ahead of him!

"*Please,* would you pen your birds," Tony asked Shelley, Matt's wife, in exasperation one day.

"They're fine," she replied. "Besides, this is all farmland."

Our lawn is far from perfect, but I do resent the implication.

We sent a polite registered letter, explaining that horses and chickens can do a lot of damage to the vegetables we depend on for food in winter and for sales. How about you fence your garden, came the reply. No offer to pay for the expense.

As luck—or not—would have it, all seventeen horses broke out the very next week. I found one in the Swiss chard just before breakfast. She was docile enough, so I tied her up in one of the back fields, well out of sight.

The phone rang. It was Dan.

"Tony, can you give me a lift to Chesterville? I have to pick up another alternator for Katrina's car."

The original alternator had blown on the way back from Ottawa the week before. Dan had replaced it, but in so doing—and with the bad luck only he seems to have with vehicles—had blown a bunch of fuses. The car was now lacking an alternator, fuel gauge, brake lights, radio, windshield wipers, dashboard lights and who knows what else. Katrina had been driving the farm truck to work, whereupon she discovered that it didn't fit into the parking garage beneath her building. She was avoiding parking lots and their $26 a day charge for oversize vehicles in favour of meters. As was bound to happen, she landed a thirty-five dollar parking fine for outstaying her welcome. Dan was lying low.

The two guys had much to discuss on the way to Chesterville and, indeed, by the time they returned, Tony was full of vim and vinegar.

"Dan had an idea," he said, crossing the road to talk to one of the horsy-folk. "Watch this."

My heart sank.

"According to county bylaws," I heard him say. "We have impounded your horse and are charging you fifty dollars a day for boarding."

Within the hour, the Ontario Provincial Police was at the front door.

"I see what you mean," said Officer Woodfine, eyeing the half-dozen or so chickens digging to China in the flowerbed right outside the window. "I wouldn't want them on my lawn either. But why did you take the horse?"

"To get their attention. We want neither the chickens nor the horses *chez nous*," we replied. "It's all about fencing and respect for your neighbours."

"You've made your point," Woodfine continued. "Release the horse since money isn't the objective here. I'll speak to Bill Sanschagrin at the Township office to see if there are any old bylaws we can enforce and I'll get back to you."

There aren't. But in the meantime, neighbourly relations have been permanently soured and Matt has penned—for lack of a better term, because the fencing is only on three sides—the chickens. It's only a matter of time before…

the pioneer spirit (and i don't mean moonshine!)

The five milk crates, chock full of pea pods, stood on the porch floor waiting patiently to be processed. Not that you'd know by this lot, but the garden had been pruned to a so-called manageable size when our commercial operation became a thing of the past. It was only early July and I had already harvested, sorted, trimmed, washed, blanched and baggied thirteen freezer bags of spinach. Pea production was at its zenith, broccoli was on the starting blocks, ready to be followed by zucchini, green beans and tomatoes.

"Hmm, do I want to shuck peas in front of the TV? Or in the sun-drenched porch?" I weighed the pros and cons of the scant entertainment provided by the few channels that came in clearly on the antenna against catching some glorious rays. The porch won out. Summer is short enough as it is.

"Ah, peas! Yum!" said Tony, passing through to the kitchen with an armful of something else in need of processing. "I love fresh peas."

"Yeah. I love them too," I smiled.

As the afternoon sun worked its way around the big ash tree in the front yard—in which two orioles were busily engaged in their own version of home construction—and began its ritual descent, the porch turned cool, then cold. I was on crate number four and my fingertips were greenish and sore. Had my thumb turned green too, at least there would have been some satisfactory simile with my gardening prowess. But no…

My mood darkened along with the fading daylight. After blanching, those five crates shrank to six freezer bags of edible product. Or measured differently, about twelve meals.

"You know, peas are a lot of work," I told Tony. "It's not that expensive to buy organic peas from the store anymore. The grocery store in Morrisburg has a really good selection of organics now."

"But we're growing our own," replied Tony. "The way the pioneers did it. There was no Loblaws back then. We're making a pretty good stab at being self-sufficient."

I'd like to meet the pioneer who can survive an Eastern Ontario winter on thirteen bags of spinach and six bags of peas.

"Just because we're not growing commercially doesn't mean we have to be pioneers instead," I said. "I like having a flushing toilet, hot water and a washing machine."

Actually, I had discovered that viable alternatives to the conventional flushing toilet do exist, but as with most things on the fringe of mainstream, they are occasionally eccentric and invariably expensive. We'd have to sacrifice the bathroom to a port-a-potty type affair that either needed regular disposal (the ad neglected to mention *where* this disposal might occur) or a massive composting chamber in the basement—flies 'n all! As for the washing machine, I wasn't prepared to contemplate any alternatives that resembled a pioneer-style washboard and wringer. Period.

"But self-sufficiency doesn't necessarily mean stepping back several centuries in hygiene and lifestyle," I continued. "I'm sure we can find a happy medium."

"Sure," replied Tony, waiting to see what I could come up with.

"Well, for a start, imagine if we did go off the grid. We'd have to find an alternative way to pump water from the well. Doing the dishes and flushing the toilet would take on a whole new meaning."

"And that's exactly why we're staying *on* the grid," said Tony. "We have to find out what we're prepared to do, what we're not prepared to do and live with our choices. Besides, I think I'd miss those god-awful stations we get on the TV."

"Right off the bat, I can tell you I'm not making any more soap. There are lots of brands now that are cruelty-free and have no animal ingredients." In my more militant days, I had learned to make soap, shampoo and a variety of face potions that met my ethical standards. It wasn't a time-consuming hobby in the city when we had nothing better to do. Out here, it was one extra thing on the to-do list.

"Well, I've split my last log. We can buy good hardwood, ready split and delivered. All we have to do is stack it." Tony was getting the hang of this as he thought of the weekend he had spent in the company of his chainsaw and Roger's log splitter. Two whole days down the drain and only two cords of wood (we need eight for an average winter), some blisters and a bloody pair of work gloves to show for it.

"And I'm done freezing peas. I'll do other veggies that take half the time instead. We'll buy our peas."

"I'm not sowing endless seeds by hand any more. We'll get that gizmo that digs a trench, puts down the seed, covers it *and* gets the spacing right. We won't have to bend over any more."

Tony and I both leaned back. We had cut our work in half. Now, we felt, there would be time to enjoy some of the joys of country living, not only the hard labour.

"To think the pioneers really did all that stuff," said Tony. "No wonder they all died young."

And that's the story of how the garden got pruned to yet another manageable size and the pioneer spirit got watered down into something the liquor store might legally sell.

reflections

Five years ago, almost to the day, Tony and I dropped our belongings on the kitchen floor of this hobby farm we had just bought and gasped in horror. Empty of the former owners' furnishings, our eyes were drawn to the flaws like ships to a beacon.

"We've bitten off more than we can chew," he muttered. "This place needs to be demolished, not renovated."

I spotted two rusty horseshoes nailed to a doorframe. This was a good omen.

"We'll take one small bite at a time," I replied. "You'll see. We'll look after the land and it will look after us."

Fast-forward to the present and what has changed? Under his tender, loving, organic care, Dan has rehabilitated the fields. The garden has been whittled away into something from which we can derive pleasure, satisfaction and a modicum of food. Nothing to be ashamed of there. The house? Well, that's about two-thirds done now. I predict it'll be a money pit until it falls into ruin, but so far, we've proved young enough, strong enough and foolish enough to give it a new lease on life. Not a bad little list.

That said, the insane workaholic days are behind us. We've been farmers; we've been pioneers; we've been renovators. Now, we're country-dwellers—settled into a routine that looks more like other people's. A routine that includes time to enjoy the bird sanctuary, the Seaway, our land, our pond, our friends and neighbours—our lifestyle.

Are we living so differently than in the city? Maybe—maybe not, but we had some great adventures to show for our efforts.